PRAISE FOR
WHY MEN HATE GOING TO CHURCH

"This is one of the most helpful books for understanding why men are indifferent toward church and how churches must change to welcome men."

— MARK DRISCOLL
Pastor of Mars Hill Church,
cofounder of Acts 29 church
planting organization; founder of
The Resurgence

"As a trainer of churches all over the world, I cannot remember one session where I have not recommended *Why Men Hate Going to Church* by David Murrow. It is a prophetic and relevant 'snap-out-of-it' masterwork that every pastor must read—not just for the sake of the kingdom, but also for his own sake and sanity in ministry. David's words are strong but needed medicine for those of us who call ourselves pastors."

— KENNY LUCK
Men's pastor, Saddleback Church

"David Murrow knows how to connect with men. Where was this guy when I was twenty?"

— FRANK PASTORE
Host of America's largest Christian
talk show, KKLA (Los Angeles)

"A church filled with committed men is unstoppable. This is the playbook that can literally redefine and rebuild the church body and its impact on men in this new season in America."

— BRAD STINE
"God's comic" comedian, actor,

"In this volume, David Murrow puts his finger on some of the key reasons why men hate the traditional form of church. This book shows us a way of 'being church' that lines up with the New Testament and reveals the stunning greatness of Christ to the world."

— Frank Viola
Author of *Pagan Christianity*,
Reimagining Church, *Jesus Manifesto*,
and *From Eternity to Here*

"David Murrow's ministry has impacted thousands of churches around the world. *Why Men Hate Going to Church* is a transforming work that will cause you to think differently about what it takes to involve men in your church."

— Dr. James Grassi
President and founder,
Men's Ministry Catalyst

"The first edition was excellent. This one's better. Everyone interested in getting men into church should read this book, read it again, and then lend it to a friend."

— Bill Perkins
Speaker; author of
The Jesus Experiment

"David Murrow has quickly become one of the leading voices in the world regarding issues of men and the church. His research is vital to any leader trying to reach men."

— Dr. Chuck Stecker
President/founder, A Chosen
Generation and Center for
InterGenerational Ministry

"In this gem of a book, David Murrow presents clear and convincing reasons for why men aren't in church. . . . *Why Men Hate Going to Church* challenges every churchgoer to step up to the plate and do what it takes to engage the men in their congregations."

— Dr. Albert L. Winseman
Faith Communities Global Practice
Leader, The Gallup Organization

"As a lifelong Catholic girl, I've often wondered why men are less than enthusiastic about church. Now I know why. *Why Men Hate Going to Church* was a real eye-opener for me."

— U.S. SENATOR LISA MURKOWSKI
(R-ALASKA)

"This is an eye-opening resource for Christians concerned with the retreat of men from the life and ministry of our churches. . . . David Murrow offers wonderful and insightful advice to help remedy this dire situation and recover the vital role of men in today's church."

— DR. GARY COOK
President, Dallas Baptist University

"Women, if you really want to know why men are so bored, uneasy, and passive in church, this is the book for you. If you want to know why he'd rather play golf than meet with the God of the universe, read this book."

— FLORENCE LITTAUER
Founder, CLASSeminar;
speaker; author of *Personality Plus*
and *Silver Boxes*

"David Murrow has made a painful reality profoundly clear: most churches no longer connect with men. Of course, it doesn't have to be that way, and Murrow shows why. But until we acknowledge the problem, nothing will change and we will lose millions of sons, husbands, and friends—and the gifts they bring to the church in the process."

— DR. ROBERT M. LEWIS
Founder, Men's Fraternity

"*Why Men Hate Going to Church* encourages and enables women to dive deeply into the hearts of men and understands what motivates them spiritually. While exposing the reality and danger of churches overrun by feminine ideals Murrow offers theological brilliance grounded in richly biblical truths. This is an amazingly insightful book."

— GINGER PLOWMAN
Author of *Don't Make Me Count to Three*

"I've often noticed that sermons on Mother's Day tend to gush over moms, while on Father's Day they tell dads to 'shape up.' I've always thought this strange, but David Murrow's book explains how common this attitude actually is. The modern church pushes men out of the pews by ignoring their needs and devaluing their stengths. For churches and individuals wondering where all the men have gone, *Why Men Hate Going to Church* gives us a much-needed diagnosis and a practical prescription to call the church back to effective, relevant ministry to America's men."

— SHEILA WRAY GREGOIRE
Author of *Honey, I Don't Have a Headache Tonight: Help for Women Who Want to Feel More "In the Mood"*

"David Murrow has shined a bright light on one of the church's darkest secrets: missing men. Church history shows that when men return to church, its impact on society multiplies. Murrow documents the reasons men are absent, then provides practical suggestions to make church a place where both men and women feel at home. You may not agree with everything Murrow says, but you can't ignore it."

— DR. WOODY DAVIS
President and head coach, TEAMinistries, Inc.

"The problem of missing men could be the most difficult challenge the church faces today. We try to fix this problem with minor program adjustments, then wonder why there is little or no change! I challenge every Christian to read this book, to understand the problem, and to enter into the battle to build spiritual fathers."

— DAN SCHAEFFER
Author, speaker, and director of Building Brothers

"Women, if you're having trouble getting Bubba off the couch and into the pew, this is the book for you. In a fair, enlightening, and entertaining manner, Murrow shares how to stand by our men, releasing them to God's great adventure, instead of taming or redecorating them."

— BECKY FREEMAN
Author and speaker

"Finally, a book that helps women understand why our best efforts to get our husbands to church almost always fail. In *Why Men Hate Going to Church*, Dave Murrow shows how we—and the church—have tried to 'feminize' men and why they fight against it (and why they should). We don't want girly men! We want men of God! Murrow believes that's possible and that it's not too late for it to happen."

— Nancy Kennedy
Author of *When He Doesn't Believe*
and *Between Two Loves*

"For every female who has ever wondered, 'Why isn't my man more into church?' For every male who has ever wondered, 'What's wrong with me?' For every leader who has ever wondered, 'How can we reach and inspire men?' David Murrow has brought to us a fresh voice regarding the spiritual gender differences and some amazing insights and stunningly simple solutions to the complex problem of reaching and inspiring the male. Though it's not likely that men were dropped on their heads in the fall, this book offers better explanations of what makes guys tick and what ticks them off. It should be a crime for the things of God to bore *anyone*, and David is a first-rate crime stopper for the spirits of the male species."

— Anita Renfroe
Comedian and author of *The Purse
Driven Life*

"And where are the men? David Murrow asks why so many good men do not fit the molds and patterns offered by the contemporary church. So should we, if we are to proclaim the gospel in its fullness."

— David Dobler
Former moderator,
Presbyterian Church (USA)

WHY MEN HATE GOING TO CHURCH

COMPLETELY REVISED AND UPDATED

DAVID MURROW

THOMAS NELSON
Since 1798

NASHVILLE   DALLAS   MEXICO CITY   RIO DE JANEIRO

Published in Nashville, Tennessee, by Thomas Nelson. Thomas Nelson is a registered trademark of Thomas Nelson, Inc.

Thomas Nelson, Inc., titles may be purchased in bulk for educational, business, fund-raising, or sales promotional use. For information, please e-mail SpecialMarkets@ThomasNelson.com.

This book is adapted from material from *Why Men Hate Going to Church* (Nashville: Thomas Nelson, 2005), *How Women Help Men Find God* (Nashville: Thomas Nelson, 2008), and other sources.

Unless otherwise marked, Scripture quotations are taken from the New King James Version. © 1982 by Thomas Nelson, Inc. Used by permission. All rights reserved.

Scripture quotations marked CEV are taken from the Contemporary English Version. © 1991 by the American Bible Society. Used by permission.

Scripture quotations marked KJV are taken from the King James Version of the Bible. Public domain.

Scripture quotations marked NIV are taken from the Holy Bible, New International Version®, NIV®. Copyright © 1973, 1978, 1984 by Biblica, Inc.™ Used by permission of Zondervan. All rights reserved worldwide. www.zondervan.com

Library of Congress Cataloging-in-Publication Data

Murrow, David.
  Why men hate going to church / David Murrow. — Completely rev. and updated.
    p. cm.
  Includes bibliographical references (p. 225–237).
  ISBN 978-0-7852-3215-5 (trade paper)
  1. Christian men—Religious life. 2. Church work with men. 3. Church attendance. I. Title.
  BV639.M4M67 2011
  277.3'083081—dc23   2011033356

Printed in the United States of America

11 12 13 14 15 QG 5 4 3 2 1

CONTENTS

INTRODUCTION

APRIL 27, 2007, I WAS THE KEYNOTE SPEAKER FOR THE PRESBYTERIAN
Church (USA) Men's Churchwide Gathering in Louisville, Kentucky.
I had been invited to speak about my new book, *Why Men Hate Going
to Church*.

I was hoping for a good crowd. The PCUSA, though in decline,
still had more than 2.6 million members. More than three thousand Presbyterian women had just wrapped up their gathering in
Louisville.

I arrived the morning of April 27 and walked down to the banquet
hall where I was to speak. I entered the room and did a double take. It
was tiny, with seating for fewer than one hundred. I checked the sign
on the door: "2007 Presbyterian Men's Churchwide Gathering." I was
in the right place.

Final score: Presbyterian women: 3,000+. Presbyterian men: 88.

o o o

You are reading a revised version of *Why Men Hate Going to Church*. I
agreed to update the book because it's needed now more than ever.
The percentage of men participating in church grows smaller each
year. The typical US worship service draws an adult crowd that's
61 percent women. Church volunteers and employees are still overwhelmingly female. Major national men's ministries such as Promise

Keepers used to pack stadiums—but now have trouble filling church auditoriums. Ethnic and overseas churches report gender gaps as high as 10 to 1. Christian colleges are becoming convents.

New research reveals the importance of men to congregational vitality and growth. Almost without exception, growing churches draw healthy numbers of men, while declining congregations lack male presence and participation.

But even as men retreat, signs of hope abound. Since I wrote the original version of this book, I've discovered a number of congregations that have shifted to a more intentional focus on men—and are prospering as a result. A few seminaries have finally begun addressing the issue of missing and passive males. Songwriters are once again composing with men in mind. And innovative ministry to men is sprouting in the most unexpected places.

Even if you are not a Christian, you have a dog in this fight. Religion is not going to disappear. Men will always seek God. The only question is, *which God will they seek?* A God of love and peace, or a God of hatred and violence? It's no coincidence that the nations in which Christianity was the freely chosen religion of men are also bastions of tolerance, charity, and political stability. And abundant research spotlights the many benefits that accrue to society and families as men engage in a local congregation.

o o o

This revision is a mashup of content from the original *Why Men Hate Going to Church*, along with newer sections plucked from *How Women Help Men Find God, The Map*, and other books and articles I've written. So if you read paragraphs that sound familiar, you may have seen them on my websites or in another one of my books. My publisher assured me that it was okay to plagiarize myself.

Also, I've trimmed this revision down to fighting weight. *Why Men* was my first book, and I didn't know if there was going to be another one. So I packed it with too much verbiage and a few rabbit trails. I've completely reorganized this new edition, adding the latest findings and examples from churches that are turning the tide. And I've created the most requested feature—a chapter-by-chapter group discussion guide. The guide is available free from my website: www .churchformen.com/guides.

I will be focusing on the practical instead of the spiritual in this book. This may come as a shock to some. I'm not saying that spiritual practices such as prayer, Bible reading, and preaching are unimportant. In fact, if God is moving in a congregation, nothing else matters much.

But we tend to ignore the practical. And it matters more than we realize. Let me illustrate.

In the early 1800s, two missionaries sailed from England for the jungles of Africa. The first missionary built an English-style church, preached in English, and imposed an English-style dress code on his African congregation. The second missionary built a church that resembled a local gathering house. He preached in the native language and allowed people to dress as they pleased.

I don't have to tell you which man met with greater success.

Both men were powerful preachers. Both were men of prayer. Both presented the gospel every week. Yet the second missionary reached many more people because he got the practical things right. He did not modify the gospel; he simply presented it in a way his hearers understood.

Men are the world's largest unreached people group. Men have a unique culture, language, and way of life. They respond differently than women. If you doubt this, simply watch the TV commercials on a men's sporting event. Then click over and watch the commercials on a women's soap opera. The ads are completely different—as if they're targeting two separate species.

Jesus called his followers to be fishers of men. My job is to show you how to get men into the net (the local church)—and keep them from jumping back into the sea. Once they're in the net, the spiritual takes precedence. Fair enough?

o o o

Seven things you will not find in this book:

1. BLAME. When the first edition of this book arrived, some condemned it for "blaming women." I thought I had been very clear, but this time let me be crystal clear: women are not to blame for the gender gap. Neither are men. Or pastors. Honestly, who cares? The purpose of this book is to illuminate the problem and seek solutions. Period.

2. "SUBMIT TO ME, WOMAN." This book is not about subjugating women or stripping them of their rights. The goal is not male dominance but male resurgence.

3. THE PHRASE "MEN SHOULD JUST . . ." This is not a book about how men ought to be. Instead, it's an honest look at how men are. It shines a light on the growing chasm between church culture and the real needs of men.

4. A CLEVER MARKETING CAMPAIGN TO GET MEN BACK. Marketing is not the answer; it is the problem. Decades of female-targeted marketing is one of the main reasons Christianity is losing its men.

5. THE OBVIOUS SOLUTIONS. Of course we'd see more men in church if pastors preached better sermons, if Christians were less hypocritical, and if everyone prayed more. This book focuses on the underlying reasons men find church distasteful—reasons you may not have considered.

6. THE ANSWER AS TO WHY AN INDIVIDUAL MAN IS NOT A CHRISTIAN. A book cannot diagnose the spiritual condition of a particular man. The reasons men reject the faith are many. This book examines the mentality of the herd, rather than the behavior or experiences of an individual bull.

7. A CALL TO COMPLETELY CHANGE THE CHURCH. Your congregation does not require an extreme makeover. There's no need for a new gospel or Jesus—the originals will work just fine. I'm convinced that in many cases, a few gentle

course corrections are all it would take for the majority of congregations to connect with more men.

o   o   o

Common story: a man has an encounter with God. He begins growing in faith. Then—*kaboom!*—he steps on a land mine. He leaves the church. His faith is destroyed.

Think of this book as a map of the minefield. I'm going to show you how to recognize the triggers, trip wires, and booby traps buried deep in Christian culture—and how to remove them.

Many have called men back to church. Now it's time to call the church back to men.

PART I

WHERE ARE THE MEN?

MY WIFE, GINA, AND I ENJOY LIVING IN ALASKA. WE TRY TO TAKE full advantage of our short but beautiful summers. So do mosquitoes. Trillions of these flying vampires bedevil our state from late May to early September.

I've noticed something odd. Mosquitoes rarely bother Gina, but they attack me like kids diving for candy under a broken piñata. Before hiking I must bathe myself in mosquito repellent; she slips on one of those coiled bracelets and goes unbitten.

Like those mosquitoes, there's something buzzing around our churches that is literally sucking the lifeblood out of our men. But women seem largely unaffected. In the next six chapters we begin identifying this pesky affliction.

Chapter 1

PERFECTLY DESIGNED

IT'S SUNDAY MORNING, AND THREE MEN ARE BUSYING THEMSELVES on Rosewood Street.

The first one is Ward. He's a welder by trade who's getting his boat ready for an afternoon of fishing with a couple of buddies. His wife, Cristin, is at church with the kids, but she's promised to stop by the store on the way home to pick up a half rack of liquid entertainment for the cooler.

Ward's next-door neighbor, Dean, is out mowing the grass. He's a thirty-one-year-old computer tech who grew up Methodist. Like many men, Dean dropped out of church as a teen. He and his wife, Maria (a lapsed Catholic), have talked about going back, since church would be good for their two kids, but it just never seems to happen.

Across the street, Peter is repairing a broken barbecue grill. He works as an engineer with the state department of transportation. His wife, Mitzi, is a faithful churchgoer, but Peter only attends on the three days of male obligation: Christmas Eve, Easter, and Mother's Day.

Ward, Dean, and Peter all believe in God. If you asked them their religion, they would confidently reply, "Christian." They would even admit to feeling a strong connection with God. All three would say they're trying their best to follow Jesus. Yet they do not go to church. Ask them why and they'll reply:

3

- Ward: "I can worship God better out in nature than I can sitting in a church building."
- Dean: "I just don't feel like I need to go to a church to be a good person."
- Peter: "I go to church on occasion, but I've found it rather boring and irrelevant to my life. I don't mind if Mitzi goes, but it's just not for me."

Ward, Dean, and Peter are decent guys. They love their wives and kids. They work hard and pay their bills. They enjoy a cold beer and a dirty joke. They're not particularly saintly or sinful. And they honestly believe they're Christians.

But church isn't on their radar. They've tried it. It didn't work for them.

While some Western men are openly hostile toward the Christian faith, I believe most are simply ambivalent toward it. What's more troubling, the men who *do* go to church seem to become more passive and detached by the day.

Men freely acknowledge the goodness of Christ. Many recognize value in the church, but they cannot see a place for themselves within it. Their time is precious, and church just doesn't provide the return on investment they're looking for. Frankly, there are better offers out there.

While there are certainly women who feel this way as well, their numbers are much smaller. Women seem to instinctively understand the purpose of church and have much less trouble finding their place within it.

So why is this happening? How can so many men who claim to know Christ hate going to church?

o o o

One Sunday I was sitting in church, half-listening to the sermon, when my wandering mind recalled a quote from a business guru: "Your system is perfectly designed to give you the results you're getting."

As I sat in that pew, I wondered, *What kind of results is this church system getting?* I looked around the sanctuary and counted noses. More than 60 percent of the adult noses had lipstick underneath. I identified at least a dozen married women whose husbands were absent, but not one married man who had come sans spouse. With the tots dismissed for junior church, there were a handful of teenage boys but almost no men between the ages of eighteen and thirty-five. Best I could tell, there was not one unmarried man in the house.

What kind of involvement was our church system producing? I studied the bulletin: all of the midweek and volunteer opportunities were pitched at women and children. Each announcement ended with "For more information, call . . ." followed by a woman's name.

I looked around at the men. Most were present in body only. Truth be told, the only man in the room who was fully engaged was the pastor, who, as he clicked past the twenty-minute mark in his sermon, seemed to be picking up steam—even as the men in the crowd were losing theirs.

I began to wonder: Could that business guru's theory apply here? What if Christianity's primary delivery system, the local church, is perfectly designed to give us the results we're getting? What if church is built to reach women, children, and elderly folks?

I've since left my traditional Presbyterian congregation and moved to one of those fast-growing megachurches. Our fellowship meets in a former warehouse space. The auditorium feels more like a theater than a sanctuary, sporting two huge video screens and a stage bathed in dimmable lighting. We've replaced the choir and organ with a rock band. My pastor no longer wears the clerical robe—instead, he's in jeans and a snap-button shirt adorned with skater-cool filigree.

This hip, modern church system delivers a higher percentage of men than my old one. Fewer than 40 percent of the adults in my Presbyterian church were male, but in my new church it's closer to 45 percent. And unlike the Presbyterians, we actually attract a fair number of young, single men.

However, all is not well. While the men of the megachurch may comprise a higher percentage of Sunday worshippers, they seem even less committed than their Presbyterian brethren. Most stand mute during the lengthy "praise and worship" sets. Few volunteer. Most are unaware that the church offers a men's ministry program.

Once, after a worship service at a megachurch, I saw a young father standing in the lobby, looking bored, while his wife chatted away with a friend. I walked up and introduced myself. His name was Gil. I asked him how long he'd been attending our church. "Well, we just started coming back to church," he said, shooting a quick glance over at his children, as if to say, *I'm here for her and the kids*. I asked him why he and his wife chose our church. In a moment of shocking honesty, he said, "We tried other churches, but this was the only one that didn't suck."

I think a lot of churchgoing men are like Gil. They sense that Christianity is a good thing—particularly for women and children. But they don't really see a compelling role for themselves within it. So they choose a church that "doesn't suck." A church with good music, decent preaching, comfortable chairs, and a service that's not too long.

A lot of men have assigned religion to their wives' basket of responsibilities. They see women as better qualified to make decisions when it comes to relationships, child care, education, and faith. These men would no sooner choose a church than choose drapes. It's just not a man's role.

o o o

This brings us back to our axiom: *your system is perfectly designed to give you the results you're getting.* The more I study churches, the more I come to believe the modern church system is engineered to reach women. Our very definition of a "good Christian" skews female. To illustrate, take this pop quiz. Examine these two sets of values, and tell me: Which set better characterizes the values of Jesus Christ and his true disciples?

Set A	Set B
Competence	Love
Power	Communication
Efficiency	Beauty
Achievement	Relationships
Skills	Support
Proving oneself	Helping
Results	Nurturing
Accomplishment	Feelings
Objects	Sharing
Goal orientation	Relating
Self-sufficiency	Community
Success	Loving cooperation
Competition	Personal expression

Over the years, I have administered this quiz to thousands of people: men and women, Christians and non-Christians. More than 90 percent of the time, people choose Set B as the best representation of Christ and his values. You probably did too.

Now comes the fun part.

These two value-sets are plucked from the best-selling book *Men Are from Mars, Women Are from Venus*. In chapter 2, Dr. John Gray identifies Set A as the values of Mars, whereas Set B describes the values of Venus.[1] In other words, Set A represents the values common among men, while Set B represents the values common among women.

This little quiz reveals a startling truth: most people think of Christ as having the values that come naturally to a woman.

Dr. Woody Davis studied this issue more formally. Davis "conducted a series of focus groups to identify the primary themes of the Christian faith. The ten most mentioned responses all came from

American culture's feminine set, including such themes as support, nurture, humility and dependence."[2] There's widespread agreement—among the religious and the irreligious alike—that genuine Christianity is, at its core, a soft, nurturing faith. To "be like Christ" means always loving, always caring, always compassionate, and always gentle. Jesus does not judge people; he hugs them.

Take another look at Set B. Any organization built upon Venus values will attract people whose gifts and skills are aligned with these values. It follows that any person, male or female, who possesses these soft skills will find his or her place in church. People who are highly verbal, musical, sensitive, and relational will fit right in.

Meanwhile, individuals, be they male or female, whose values and skills skew toward Mars will have a harder time integrating into the local church, because these are not generally seen as useful to (or even compatible with) Christ.

Now, I must acknowledge the obvious—there are many men who are quite comfortable in the church. You're probably thinking of Stan, who leads mission trips overseas. Or Roger, who teaches the boys' Sunday school class. Or Liam, the worship pastor. Or Anthony, who stands in the front row with holy hands lifted in praise. And of course, you're thinking of Pastor Chuck, one of the saintliest men on planet Earth.

Why do these men fit in so well at church? In many cases, church fits them. Highly involved churchmen often possess the Venus values. I'm not calling these men effeminate; I'm pointing out that men who are particularly drawn to church are often highly verbal, sensitive, and relational. They're wonderful guys who are comfortable with church as it is. They tend to dismiss any effort to restore masculinity to the church as a "pandering to macho men." They are comfortable in church—and can't imagine why another man wouldn't be.

In summary: The church system is perfectly designed to reach a certain type of person. There are men and women who fit this type, but women are the majority. Therefore, there are more women in church. This creates a vicious circle:

church culture built
on Venus values

more women than men
possess these values

more women get
involved in church

surplus of women
pushes the church
toward Venus values

As a congregation becomes ever more focused on Venus ways of knowing, thinking, and ministering, power flows to men who know how to function in an environment dominated by feminine gifts and values. Men who are verbal, studious, musical, and sensitive rise to the top. They get the "stage time," while average Joes who lack these soft virtues either leave the church or become passive pew sitters. (In chapter 11 we'll see why some men shine while others sulk in church.)

o   o   o

Men don't hate God or Christ or the Bible or Christianity. They hate a system that's perfectly designed to reach someone else. A system that makes them feel unneeded. A system that exalts the gifts they simply do not possess. As Albert Einstein once said, "Everybody is a genius. But if you judge a fish by its ability to climb a tree, it will live its whole life believing that it is stupid."

Discussion questions for this chapter are available free at www.churchformen.com/guides.

Chapter 2

YES, THERE REALLY
IS A GENDER GAP

ONE DAY I GOT A CALL FROM A REPORTER WITH THE *PHILADELPHIA Inquirer.* After a spirited interview, she asked, "Do you know of any churches in Philadelphia that have a gender gap?"

I'd never been to Philly, so I took a guess. "According to the research, African-American congregations suffer the largest gaps," I said. "Look up an AME or Church of God in Christ, and give them a call."

About a week later, the reporter called me with a fascinating story to tell. "I spoke with an AME elder about his church's gender gap. He assured me that his congregation had equal numbers of men and women. However, he promised to make an actual head count on Sunday."

The reporter continued, "First thing Monday morning the elder called, upset. 'I owe you an apology, ma'am,' he said, voice shaking. 'I counted every adult—and we had five times as many women in church as men. Five times! It's been this way for years—and I'd never noticed.'"

o o o

For years the experts have told us the church is a men's club. Feminists condemn the church as patriarchal and male dominated. Reformers complain that the language of the Bible and hymns is sexist and excludes women. Liberals accuse certain churches of oppressing women by refusing to allow them to become pastors or elders. The media have a field day anytime a church leader utters the word *submission*.

In the church, men have always been in charge. Christianity was founded by a man and his twelve male associates. Ninety-five percent of the senior pastors in America are men.[1] Every Catholic priest, bishop, cardinal, and pope is a man. Some church boards are composed entirely of men. Christians sit in church, look up and see a man in the pulpit, and assume the institution he leads is a bastion of male power and privilege.

But look beyond the relatively thin stratum of professional clergy, and you find a church dominated by women and their values. Dr. Leon Podles says it well: "Modern churches are women's clubs with a few male officers."[2]

Whenever large numbers of Christians gather, men are never in the majority. Not at revivals. Not at crusades. Not at conferences. Not at retreats. Not at concerts. With the exception of men's events and pastoral conferences, can you think of any large gathering of Christians that attracts more men than women?

Visit a church during the week and you'll find most of the people working there are female. Drop in on a committee meeting and you'll find a majority of the volunteers are women—unless it's that small bastion of male presence, the building committee. Look over the leadership roster: the pastor is likely to be a man, but at least two-thirds of his ministry leaders will be women.[3] Examine the sign-up sheets for volunteer work, prayer, Sunday school, and nursery duty. You'll be lucky to see more than a couple of men's names on these lists.

Male ministers come and go, but faithful women provide a matriarchal continuity in our congregations. Women are the devoted ones who build their lives around their commitments to Christ and his church. Women are more likely to teach and volunteer in church and are the greatest participants in Christian culture. The sad reality in many congregations is this: the only man who actually practices his faith is the pastor.

Women are the pack mules of modern Christianity, but people still think church is a men's club. Why is this?

Humans tend to be misled by something I call the *man-in-charge fallacy*. They look at an organization's leader and assume he reflects the rank and file. For example, 97 percent of Fortune 500 CEOs are male, so we assume that the business world is male dominated. However, American firms now employ more women than men.[4] Businesswomen are quickly gaining parity in power, pay, and perks. The same is true in music—the world's most famous recording artists are mostly male, but women are far more likely to play an instrument or possess formal musical training. When we think of a chef, we picture a rotund man in a tall, white hat, yet women do most of the cooking at home.

o o o

Are men forsaking the church for atheism? Not here in the United States. According to polls, 90 percent of American men claim belief in God. Five out of six call themselves Christians. But just two out of six US men claim to have attended church in the previous week.[5] Some experts believe the true number is fewer than one in six.[6] Churches in other countries suffer gender gaps as high as 10 to 1.[7]

For decades those few people who noticed the gender gap have assumed that men are to blame for it. Sometimes they are. Many men intentionally reject the Christian faith. Some men are proud and want to be their own god. Men hate to admit weakness or neediness. Millions are captive to sin, unbelief, and other religions that preclude commitment to Christ. Men get distracted by the concerns of this world and lose interest in spiritual matters. Men suffer abuse at the hands of church people and fall away.

But let's be honest—women grapple with these same issues. Women are just as susceptible to sin, atheism, other religions, and pride. There's nothing in the Bible to suggest that women are more virtuous or less sinful than men. Women are just as likely to have father issues or suffer abuse in the church.

Men's disinterest in Christianity is so consistent around the world, it can't be explained by pride, father issues, sin, or distraction. Neither can we say, "Men are just less religious," because this is untrue. Male and female participation are roughly equal in Judaism, Buddhism, and

Hinduism. In the Islamic world men are publicly and unashamedly religious—often more so than women. Of the planet's great religions, only Christianity has a consistent, worldwide shortage of male practitioners.

o   o   o

So who goes to church? Women. The US Congregational Life Survey pegged the typical churchgoer as a fifty-year-old, married, well-educated, employed female.[8] An ABC News/Beliefnet poll found that a worshipper is most likely an older, black female who lives in the South.[9] By combining figures from the US Census and a study by Barna Research, we can estimate a weekly gender gap of more than thirteen million in America's churches.[10]

Adult women in church	48,660,177
Adult men in church	35,348,028
Gap size	13,312,149

The US Congregational Life Survey concurs: "While the U.S. population is split fairly evenly between men and women, there are more women (61%) than men (39%) in the pews. This difference is found in every age category, so the fact that women live longer than men does not explain the gender difference in religious participation."[11]

Almost a quarter of America's married, churchgoing women regularly attend without their husbands.[12] Step into any church parking lot, and you're likely to see an attractive young mother and her brightly scrubbed children scurrying to Sunday school. Mom may be wearing an impressive diamond ring on her left hand, but the man who gave it to her is nowhere to be seen.

WHICH CHURCHES HAVE THE BIGGEST GAPS?

This section highlights some results from the National Congregations Study (NCS).[13] The NCS first surveyed the church in 1998 and came back for a second wave in 2006–2007. Comparing the two sets of data, we discover a disturbing trend: the exodus of men from the church is accelerating.

To conform to the findings of the NCS, any congregation with at least 12 percent more women than men will be considered "gender gapped." So for our purposes, a gapped congregation looks like this:

A "gender-gapped" congregation draws an adult crowd that is 56 percent or more female.

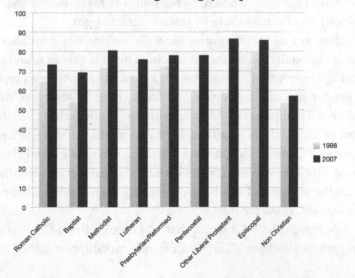

Percent of churches with gender gaps, by denomination

The gender gap engulfed many more congregations during the nine-year span between surveys. For example, in 1998, 55 percent of Baptist churches reported a gender gap. Nine years later, 69 percent did. Twenty percent more Pentecostal churches reported a gap in 2007. Liberal mainline denominations also saw dramatic increases in the number of congregations reporting a man shortage. An astonishing 85 percent of Episcopal churches now report a gender gap.

These numbers suggest the gender gap and church decline go hand in hand. Mainline denominations such as Lutheran, Presbyterian, Methodist, Church of Christ, and Episcopal have been hemorrhaging members for decades, and they are also very likely to be short on men.

These figures also point to the denominational loyalty of women. Men are absenting themselves from all kinds of churches, but they seem particularly disenchanted with the established denominations. In many cases faithful women are keeping the doors of these traditional churches open, but with scant male participation they seem unable to reverse the fortunes of their congregations.

The Catholic Church is having a particularly hard time attracting men. An ABC News/Beliefnet poll found that just 26 percent of US Catholic men attend Mass on a weekly basis, compared to 49 percent of Catholic women.[14] This poll was taken before the worst allegations of sexual abuse by priests came to light.

But, as I told that reporter in Philly, no one has it tougher than the traditionally black denominations. The 1998 survey found a staggering 92 percent of African-American churches in America reported a gender gap, the highest of any faith group.[15] Observers such as Edward Thompson and Jawanza Kunjufu confirm that 75 to 90 percent of the adults who attend African-American congregations are women.[16] Contrast this to black Muslims, who are overwhelmingly male.[17] If current trends continue, the African-American community faces the prospect of separate religions for each gender: Christianity for women, Islam for men.

Although the NCS found that 57 percent of non-Christian congregations also have a surplus of female worshippers, other studies have indicated that non-Christian groups in the US, such as atheists, freethinkers (a form of atheism), agnostics, Muslims, Buddhists, Jews, and those practicing no religion, attract more men than women.[18]

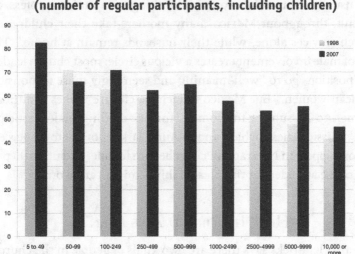

Percent of churches with gender gaps, by size (number of regular participants, including children)

Generally speaking, the smaller the church, the more likely it is to experience a gender gap. Micro churches of fewer than fifty people have the hardest time reeling in men. But the more "mega" the church, the more likely it is to have men in attendance. Nonetheless, churches of almost every size are more likely to experience a gender gap today than in 1998.

NOT JUST AN AMERICAN PHENOMENON

The gender gap exists all over the world. Although some evidence suggests that Eastern and Greek Orthodox churches in Europe and Asia do not suffer a gender gap, every other branch of Christianity does. No variant of Catholic or Protestant church is immune. Research finds a pattern of male absence going back at least a century in the churches of England, Wales, Spain, Germany, and France.

Asian, Australian, and African churches also attract more women than men on a typical weekend.[19]

The gender gap now threatens to stall the explosive growth of evangelical and Pentecostal churches in Latin America. Joshua Georgen of Latin America Mission notes, "Following Jesus Christ isn't usually seen as the most macho thing for a man to profess. As a result, throughout Mexico many mothers take their children to church services alone, while their husbands remain at home." The lack of male involvement creates a vicious circle: most church leadership positions go to "well-meaning and seemingly more responsible Mexican women." But Mexico's machista culture makes it difficult for men to be subject to women, further eroding male participation.[20] Missionaries Richard and Jo Ann Clark report 60 to 80 percent of worshippers in Nicaraguan churches are female, and up to 90 percent of the attendees at their leadership seminars are women.[21]

HOW INVOLVED ARE MEN?

Howard Hendricks says there are two kinds of people in the church: the pillars and the caterpillars. The pillars uphold the church with their prayers, their work, and their donations. They build the kingdom of God by the sweat of their brows. The caterpillars crawl in on Sunday morning, sing a few songs, listen to a sermon, and crawl out again, not to be seen for a week.

If your church is typical, most of the pillars that uphold it are female. Women are much more likely than men to devote themselves to Christianity beyond simple church attendance. Researcher George Barna found that women are:

- 100 percent more likely to be involved in discipleship;
- 57 percent more likely to participate in adult Sunday school;
- 56 percent more likely to hold a leadership position at a church (not including the role of pastor);
- 54 percent more likely to participate in a small group;

- 46 percent more likely to disciple others;
- 39 percent more likely to have a devotional time or quiet time;
- 33 percent more likely to volunteer for a church;
- 29 percent more likely to read the Bible;
- 29 percent more likely to attend church;
- 29 percent more likely to share faith with others;
- 23 percent more likely to donate to a church;
- 16 percent more likely to pray.[22]

Women put more faith in their religion, according to a study by the Gallup organization. American women agreed far more often than men when given these statements about their spiritual lives:[23]

	Men	Women
Religion is very important in my life.	48	68
I'm a member of a church or synagogue.	59	69
Religion can answer today's problems.	59	72
When making decisions, I pay attention to God.	40	56
When making decisions, I pay attention to my own views.	54	37

In addition, 38 percent of men described themselves as spiritual but not religious, compared with just 28 percent of women, suggesting that "traditional religious institutions may be somewhat less equipped to fulfill the spiritual needs of men."[24]

The Gallup organization's Congregational Engagement Index measures the commitment of individuals to their particular faith community. Not surprisingly, 28 percent of women are fully engaged in the life of their church versus 21 percent of men. Actively disengaged members are the opposite: 24 percent of men are actively disengaged versus just 16 percent of women.[25]

The most interesting finding was that women are more scriptural in their beliefs than men. Barna concludes, "The survey data show that nearly half of the nation's women have beliefs which classify them as born again (46%), compared to just about one-third of men (36%). In other words, there are between eleven million and thirteen million more born again women than there are born again men in the country."[26]

Women are also more likely to share their faith with another person and to provide spiritual mentoring to others. Women are doing the legwork of evangelism today and fulfilling the Great Commission while men sit on the sidelines. Barna sums up his findings: "Women are the backbone of the Christian congregations in America."[27]

DENOMINATIONAL AND PARACHURCH ORGANIZATIONS ATTRACT MORE WOMEN

Women's organizations within churches are much stronger than their men's counterparts. Almost every Southern Baptist congregation has a WMU (Woman's Missionary Union). There is no equivalent Baptist men's organization that comes close in size or influence. Same with the United Methodist Women, who outnumber the United Methodist Men 875,000 to 248,000.[28]

Bible Study Fellowship (BSF) International is the world's premier parachurch Bible study program. It offers three to five times more classes for women. Here are numbers from five states in different parts of the country:[29]

State	Women's Classes	Men's Classes
Texas	80	25
Massachusetts	2	0
Illinois	24	6
Washington	40	11
South Carolina	10	3

BSF's gender gap also shows up in different regions of the world:

Region	Women's Classes	Men's Classes
Canada	17	5
Great Britain	9	1
India	8	6
China	5	3
Australia	27	7
Africa	19	10

o o o

No institution more vividly illustrates the decline of male interest than Promise Keepers. In the mid-1990s, PK was filling stadiums across the country, reaching hundreds of thousands of men. It had a multi-million-dollar budget and a staff of hundreds. In 1995, more than sixty thousand men jammed the Minneapolis Metrodome for a PK men's rally. Five years later, just sixteen thousand gathered in Minneapolis's much-smaller Target Center. By 2008, Promise Keepers downsized its events again, cancelling one arena event and moving the rest to large church sanctuaries, drawing about two thousand men to each. And in 2010, PK had just one "classic" arena event, drawing a few thousand men from around the country to Denver.[30]

Meanwhile, the PK-inspired Women of Faith conferences show no signs of decline. WOF continues to sell out fifteen-thousand-seat venues in all regions of the country. If my math skills are right, it looks as if Women of Faith conferences now outdraw Promise Keepers by almost 100 to 1. And so it goes . . .

Chapter 3

MEN: WHO NEEDS 'EM?

CHURCH INVOLVEMENT IS GOOD FOR MEN. BUT SINCE WHEN DO men do what's good for them? Men regard churchgoing like a prostate exam: it's something that can save their lives, but it's so unpleasant and invasive, they put it off. Others see the worship service as their weekly dose of religion, a bitter elixir they must swallow to remain healthy, but not something to look forward to.

So men avoid church—and suffer for it. Men are more likely than women to be arrested, die violently, commit and be victims of crimes, go to jail, and be addicted. They also die more often on the job, have more heart attacks, commit suicide in greater numbers, and live shorter lives than women. I could go on.

If men want to avoid these pathologies, they should go to church. Studies indicated that churchgoers are more likely to be married and express a higher level of satisfaction with life. Church involvement is the most important predictor of marital stability and happiness. It moves people out of poverty. It's also correlated with less depression, more self-esteem, and greater family and marital happiness.[1] Religious participation leads men to become more engaged husbands and fathers.[2] Teens with religious fathers are more likely to say that they enjoy spending time with their dads and that they admire them.[3]

Obviously, men need the church. But does the church need men? Not really.

Honestly, men don't play a large role in the spiritual life of the church. They don't volunteer or participate as much. If every man (except the pastor) left on a weekend retreat, most churches would probably chug along with women covering a few empty slots. But imagine the chaos if every woman took Sunday off.

So why not leave the church to women? Why even try to get men back?

Because the church needs men.

Researcher C. Kirk Hadaway of Hartford Seminary studied more than fourteen thousand congregations and found a strong statistical link between the gender gap and church decline. "Even when controlling for the proportion of older participants, a higher proportion of women in the congregation is associated with decline rather than growth." On the flip side, churches that drew a majority of men were three times more likely to be growing than those that were majority female.[4]

After studying religion in America for more than fifty years, George Gallup concludes, "Women may be the backbone of a congregation, but the presence of a significant number of men is often a clear indicator of spiritual health."[5]

It's a great mystery: on the surface, men seem to be more trouble than they're worth. Most men are not as outwardly caring or as biblically literate as women. Some become power hungry, controlling, or even abusive. And there are always a couple of men who criticize the pastor's every move or think they could do a better job in the pulpit.

Yet despite their many flaws, there's something about men that brings vitality to a congregation. Just as a flu shot causes momentary pain but promotes long-term health, the exercise of masculine gifts may cause a congregation to be momentarily less nurturing, tender, and supportive. However, over the long term, men and their "go for it" spirit promotes health in many different ways.

MEN BRING A RISK ORIENTATION

Men are hard-wired for risk taking—particularly young men. The number one killer of fifteen- to twenty-four-year-old males is accidents.[6] Female investors hold less risky investment portfolios than their male counterparts and generally take fewer chances with their money.[7]

Churches need men because men are natural risk takers—and they bring that orientation into the church. Congregations that do not take risks atrophy. Jesus made it clear that risk taking is necessary to please God. In the parable of the talents, the master praises two servants who risked their assets and produced more, but he curses the servant who played it safe. He who avoids all risk is, in the words of Jesus, "wicked and lazy."[8]

MEN EXALT THE RULES

Men tend to exalt rules over relationships, whereas women tend to exalt relationships over rules. The great debates that have divided the mainline denominations reflect this dichotomy: conservatives (led by men) believe rules come first; liberals (led by women) believe relationships do. Liberals, out of the purest of motives, want to weaken or reinterpret biblical rules so everyone can feel loved and accepted.[9] But this is a well-worn trail of tears. Congregations that abandon the rules lose members.[10]

Men tend to be more orthodox in belief. Their concern for the rules keeps a congregation from drifting toward mushy moral relativism. Denominations that have remained doctrinally orthodox have either grown or held steady since the 1990s, but theologically liberal churches have endured steep declines.[11] The National Congregations Study found that self-described liberal churches were 14 percent more likely to have a gender gap than conservative ones.[12]

MEN IMPART STRENGTH

Edwin Louis Cole says, "You can derive spirituality from women in the church, but you get strength from the men."[13] Not a very politically correct statement, but what does your experience tell you? Doesn't the presence of spiritually alive men bring strength to the body? Gordon Dalbey notes, "A unique and truly awesome power arises when men gather together: the power which God gives especially to men collectively, to get His work done in the world."[14]

Men Bring Money

A straight-shooting pastor once told me, "When Sally comes to church and Sam doesn't, you get the tithe off the grocery money. When they come together, you get the tithe off the paycheck." A Gallup study found that people who are actively engaged in their local church give three times as much as those who are disengaged.[15] Conceivably, a church could triple its contributions just by engaging men.

Men Attract Women

Women seem to love to worship in the presence of enthusiastic men. Once a church gets a healthy crop of males, it's not long before women begin showing up in large numbers. It's hard to close the gender gap in these churches because, even as men trickle in, women pour in faster.

o o o

Christianity is still growing worldwide, but it is losing ground to two aggressive competitors: secularism and Islam.

Secularism is the de facto religion in much of Europe today. Rationalism, materialism, anarchy, and environmental extremism are a few of its common guises. It's on the rise in America as well. A study from Trinity College found the number of adults who say they subscribe to no religion rose from 8 to 15 percent between 1990 and 2008. Twenty-two percent of young adults are religious "nones," suggesting secularism will expand rapidly in coming generations.[16]

Islam is the world's fastest-growing religion—and not coincidentally, it's also wildly popular with men. Since 1950 the number of Christians in the world has doubled, but the number of Muslims has more than tripled.[17] In the US, Islam has made its strongest inroads in the African-American community. More than 90 percent of the converts to Islam in the United States are African-American men, such as Suleiman Azia. He grew up in a Baptist church in Tennessee but turned to Islam as an adult. His chief reason: his church was attended mostly by women. "In Islam I found a stronger ideal of brotherhood and moral discipline—and of manhood," Azia says.[18]

o   o   o

Why are secularism and Islam on the rise? Both have proven their ability to capture the hearts of men. In spiritual matters children have always followed their fathers. In all of human history, no religion has prospered without the robust participation and leadership of men. The religion that wins men, wins.

Chapter 4

WHO ARE THE MISSING MEN?

IN FOOTBALL, 45 POINTS IS USUALLY ENOUGH TO WIN A GAME. But not when the other team scores 51. That's exactly what happened when my favorite team, the Green Bay Packers, lost a first-round playoff game to the Arizona Cardinals in 2010.

After that heartbreaking defeat, everyone knew the Pack had an explosive offense—to go with a Swiss-cheese defense. The front office brought in some new players and changed some defensive sets. In 2011, the Packers rode their vastly improved defense all the way to a Super Bowl title.

Like the Packers of 2010, the church has plenty of strengths. Churches are great at worshipping. Gathering. Loving people. Caring for the less fortunate. Prayer.

But there are glaring weaknesses as well. Churches are timid. Focused inward. Amateurish. Stuck.

The church needs to bring in some new players who are strong where it is weak. I've identified three subsets of men who would bring great strength, if only they were on the team.

HIGH-ACHIEVING MEN ARE MISSING

In the 1950s and '60s, the governing boards of mainline churches were a who's who of community leaders. These all-male boards were composed of prominent doctors, lawyers, businessmen, bankers, and professionals. Under the leadership of these men, mainline churches exploded in size and influence.

Today, such men have not only stepped away from leadership—they are opting out of church altogether. Many of society's most powerful Christian men don't go to church at all, according to Dr. Michael Lindsay, who interviewed 360 of America's most prominent evangelicals, 90 percent of whom were men. These well-known believers included athletes, CEOs, Hollywood stars, and two US presidents. Lindsay "was shocked to find that more than half—60%—had low levels of commitment to their denominations and congregations. Some were members in name only; others had actively disengaged from church life."

Lindsay found these high-achieving men typically practiced their faith alone or in small groups, far from the public eye. He writes, "Executives and politicians are often distressed by the way churches are run. James Unruh, who served as the chief executive of Unisys, was also at one time an elder at his Presbyterian church in California. He has since decided he will never serve again. He couldn't stand the inefficiency of church meetings, a common refrain among those I interviewed. Others described local congregations as 'unproductive' and 'focused on the wrong things.'

"These factors are driving evangelical leaders into the arms of fellowship groups that exist outside the churches, often called 'parachurch' organizations," Lindsay says. "The shift began in the 1950s, but it grew dramatically over the past twenty years as the parachurch sector became more professional and well-resourced. Nearly three-fourths of the leaders I interviewed serve on the board of at least one parachurch organization, such as the Billy Graham Evangelistic Association. They prefer these groups because they have a broader reach and a bigger impact."[1]

YOUNG, SINGLE MEN ARE MISSING

Young, single men are the demographic least likely to populate the pews (just ask the young, single women). Women tell me the dating situation for Christian women is bleak here in the US—and even worse overseas. I spoke to a Christian woman from France who said, "Once a woman receives Jesus here, she is unmarriageable. There are almost no men in my country who are following Christ. And French men will not marry a woman whose faith in Jesus is so strong. She is a leper in their eyes."

Camerin Courtney writes, "A male coworker recently told me about a college visit he made with his teenage daughter. Apparently she ruled out the Christian campus they were checking out when she discovered the female-to-male ratio is two-to-one. Sadly, this isn't an uncommon phenomenon for Christian colleges."[2]

The next chapter explains in detail why young, single men avoid church. And I've devoted two chapters to the faith of young men (chapters 14 and 21).

HIGHLY MASCULINE MEN ARE MISSING

Studies show that men who are interested in Christianity have a less masculine outlook on life than other men. The church has a reputation for attracting gentle, artistic, bookish guys who are less masculine than average.

Is there any truth to this? Dr. Leon Podles cites a study by psychologists Lewis M. Terman and Catharine Cox Miles. The pair presented a set of questions to men and women. They studied how each gender answered the questions; responses that were most often chosen by women were deemed feminine, and those most often chosen by men were deemed masculine.

Men who expressed an interest in art or religion were more likely to answer like a woman than other men. In other words, the answers of artistic and religious men looked more like the answers given by women. The researchers wrote, "Interest in religion or art is a mark of definitely greater femininity than lack of interest in these matters." They continued, "Most masculine of all are the men who have little or no interest in religion." Podles observes, "Very masculine men showed little interest in religion, very feminine men great interest."

Now here's a surprise: the pattern held with women too. Women who had highly feminine scores were also especially religious, while women who had more masculine scores were neutral or averse to religion.[3]

This study seems to indicate that anyone who tends toward masculinity, whether male or female, tends to shy away from the church. Isn't this true in your experience? Think of the macho men you know. Think of the driven, career-oriented women you know. Are they in church on Sunday? Even if they do attend, do they seem particularly devout, or is their true allegiance elsewhere?

On the other hand, those who have a less masculine outlook, be they men or women, tend to flock to the church. This may explain why so many gay men are drawn to church, while lesbians avoid it. A study published in the *Journal for the Scientific Study of Religion* found that "gay men were significantly more active in religious organizations [as a percentage] when compared to heterosexual men." The author notes that gay men are similar to female heterosexuals in their religiosity and attend church "without having to be dragged to services by female partners—as is the case for heterosexual men." Yet "lesbians and female bisexuals have very low rates of religious activity."[4]

Why do so many effeminate and gay men attend church? Maybe because the church is one of the few institutions in society where there's no pressure to act like a man. In fact, men are encouraged not to. Where else can a man express his feminine side and be applauded for it?

Furthermore, as men get older and more sedentary, they tend to develop a more feminine outlook on life, focusing on security rather than risk taking. These are precisely the men the church is still somewhat successful in attracting. Mostly absent in church are young, athletic, and uneducated men, who possess a more masculine outlook on life. (See chapter 21 for a chart of male church involvement by age.)

o o o

Why are these three subgroups of men underrepresented in church? Sometimes it's the men's fault. Christ spoke of good seed being sown among thorns. Self-powered men often allow the temptations of this world to choke out spiritual pursuits.

But in many cases, men's absence reflects a deep frustration with the way churches operate. Consider these five:

Churches Value Stability and Security

In a world of constant change, the church is an anchor of stability, predictability, and tradition. In a dangerous and risky world, it is a sanctuary of safety and protection. In a world of conflict, the church is a place of peace, harmony, and comfort. Churches talk about being adventurous, but they're actually in the business of providing believers with security. Every pastor can tell you stories of members who've become hysterical over minor changes to a worship service. You might say that today's church is full of passivity activists whose greatest energies are devoted to fighting change.

Women and the elderly are more security oriented than men and young people. This is why we see so many women and old folks in church. They're in the market for security. But the missing men are looking for adventure, risk, independence, and reward. If they can't find these things in church, they'll look elsewhere.

Decisions Are Made the Feminine Way

Being a church leader is a frustrating experience, because a man cannot lead like a man. Instead he must be careful, sentimental, and thrifty; make every decision by consensus; talk everything to death. Decisions take months or years to make, and if someone's feelings might be hurt, we don't move forward.

Conflict Is Handled the Feminine Way

When two church members get crossways, do they settle it like men? Have you ever heard an elder say to a deacon, "Henry, let's step outside and settle things, mano a mano"? Of course not. Most Christians would view a fistfight among believers as terribly unchristian behavior.

Even a sharp public exchange of words is considered a horrible failure, something to be avoided at all costs.

But conflict always comes, and how does the church handle it 99 percent of the time? The feminine way, allowing it to simmer just below the surface. The battling parties are polite in public but vicious in private. Church battles routinely feature backstabbing, gossip mongering, and revenge. All this takes place in secret, and only church insiders know the details. Publicly, everyone grits his teeth and pretends things are just fine. Eventually, one warring party leaves the church, or in extreme cases the congregation splits.

Men can't handle this. When a man gets drawn into a church catfight, he's out of his league. His heart tells him to fight it out, clear the air, and move on. But that's not how things work in most churches. So men fall away. There are legions of men who have given up on church because it handles conflict the feminine way.

The Right Choice Is Always the Soft One

Before he became president of the United States, Teddy Roosevelt was a Sunday school teacher. One day a boy showed up for class with a black eye. He admitted he'd been fighting—on the Sabbath, no less. Another boy was pinching his sister, so he took a swing at the scoundrel. The future president told the boy he was proud of him and gave him a dollar. When word of this got around the church, Roosevelt was let go.

TR was caught between two scriptural imperatives: turn the other cheek and defend the weak. One soft, the other tough. He chose to praise the boy for his tough response but was fired for it, because in most churches the right choice is always the soft one.

Lack of Productivity

One New Year's Eve I asked my pastor a straightforward question: "How many adults came to faith in Christ at our church this year?" The pastor, a very diplomatic man, said, "I'm not sure. I'll have to get back to you on that." But he and I knew the answer. It was zero. I added it up. That year our church conducted 104 regularly scheduled worship services, 7 special services, some 250 adult classes, 600 committee meetings, and 1,000 small-group meetings and ran through a $750,000 budget to produce exactly 0 new adult followers of Jesus Christ.

Christ promised his faithful followers a hundredfold crop[5]—but our church hadn't even reaped a onefold crop. We gathered. We worshipped. We loved one another. But we produced no crop. Our church was a contraption worthy of Rube Goldberg: lots of sound, motion, and fury to produce a tiny amount of fruit.

How do churches conceal this scandalous lack of productivity? Some clever congregations have simply changed the definition of *crop*. Churches now judge success by the standards of a family reunion: (1) How many people came? and (2) Did everyone get along? A big, happy crowd equals a crop. The more meeting, gathering, and loving that take place, the more abundant the crop. This is another way the modern church reflects the feminine heart—*the people gathered, formed the body of Christ, and loved one another.*

Why are churches so unproductive? They try to be all things to all people. They can't say no. They do too much and end up doing a lot of things poorly. They keep adding ministry programs but never prune the ineffective ones. But parachurch organizations do one thing—such as hunger relief, housing for the poor, vaccinations, or Bible translation—and do it very well. Productivity fires the imaginations of men.

In Genesis, God gave Adam the first job—produce a crop. Ever since, men have longed to be productive. That's why many are abandoning the local church and investing their talents elsewhere. Their time is valuable, and they want to spend it on something that gets results. Can we blame them?

Chapter 5

THE MASCULINITY BANK

SOME TIME AGO, MILLER BREWING CREATED AN UNUSUAL SERIES of television commercials titled Man Laws. The ads featured macho men (athletes, coaches, wrestlers, cowboys, and he-man actors such as Burt Reynolds) sitting around a square table, debating the bounds of acceptable male behavior.

Some of the man laws included:

- Men do not iron blue jeans.
- Men do not leave a sporting event early.
- Hugs between men are acceptable, as long as only one arm is used.
- Dating your best friend's ex-girlfriend is allowed after a six-month waiting period.
- When toasting, men do not clink bottles at the top. (Saliva might be exchanged, which is almost like kissing.)

Miller took the opposite tack on its next campaign—it ridiculed "girlie men" who violate the man laws. These ads laughed at men carrying purses, being protected by their mothers, and sporting "tramp stamp" tattoos on their posteriors. The ads also mocked men for wearing womanly attire such as skirts, skinny jeans, and thong underwear. At the end of each sight gag, a deep-voiced announcer growled, "Man *up!*"

"Being manly" is a universal obsession among men. Every culture on earth has its own set of man laws. Men who follow these laws are treated with respect, but violators are ostracized, ridiculed, and rejected by their peers.

It all seems so silly. Why are men driven to be manly? Where does this need come from? Why do the man laws exist?

Without man laws, civilization would crumble.

o o o

Every society needs people to do the dangerous jobs. Throughout human history, someone has had to fight wars, travel long distances without the comforts of home, and hunt down dangerous animals. Today we need people to work in mines, rush into burning buildings, and catch bad guys.

Men have always done the dangerous jobs, and they still do them. Today 94 percent of occupational deaths occur to men.[1] Men also do most of the dying for their country. If any civilization is to survive and prosper, it needs men who will act like men when the need arises. If men are cowardly, craven, or criminal, chaos reigns.

But how do you convince men to sacrifice themselves? How do you keep a man from deserting the battle when he's scared out of his mind, from running away when an animal tries to kill him, or from sneaking back to camp when food is running low or he's freezing cold? Man laws.

Man laws are an informal code imposed on all the men of society, except for the very young and very old. A "real man" must stand up to danger, bear up under suffering, and sacrifice himself for the good of others. This code of conduct helps a man overcome his natural instincts (fear, hunger, loneliness, etc.), so he will do what's best for the tribe, not for himself. Masculine qualities such as bravery, stoicism, and self-sacrifice don't come naturally to a man; they are drawn from this cultural well.

If a man fails to be brave, stoic, or self-sacrificing, he's branded a coward. He becomes an outcast. He suffers total rejection.[2] This may seem cruel, but remember, society's very survival has always depended on men who would fulfill their roles. And this transmits a powerful lesson to the boys: be a man, or you will be rejected.

But here's the rub: masculinity isn't something you switch on and off. If a man is going to stand tough in the face of danger, he needs rehearsal time. Heroism is unnatural, and it must be practiced. Just as an Olympic sprinter works out day after day, year after year, for a race that's over in a few seconds, a man practices masculinity every day so when the time comes to be strong, he's ready.

Manhood is something a man earns. One deed at a time, a task at a time, an interaction at a time. Anthropologist David Gilmore puts it this way: "Real manhood differs from simple anatomical maleness, that it is not a natural condition that comes about spontaneously through biological maturation but rather is a precarious or artificial state that boys must win against powerful odds."[3]

o   o   o

Here's a helpful word picture: Every man carries within himself a masculinity bank. Each time he succeeds in a manly endeavor, a few coins drop into his bank: *ka-ching, ka-ching.*

For most men, the bank can never be filled. A man will begin collecting coins around age seven and will spend his entire lifetime gathering them (although the pursuit may become less consuming later in life). Men don't know they have a masculinity bank; they just know it's important to do things that are manly in the eyes of their peers.

Not all men are macho, so individual men fill their banks differently. For example, Rob the corporate executive proves his masculinity by having a corner office, complete with an attractive, young secretary. This would mean nothing to Louis the artist, who measures his masculinity by winning awards for his exceptional paintings. But artistic skill means nothing to Tom the police officer, who proves his masculinity by being the best marksman on the force. However, Kenneth the college professor has never touched a gun. He proves his masculinity by charming female students into bed with him.

Is there a positive side to all this manhood proving? Of course. It produces bravery, heroism, generosity, self-sacrifice, and innovation. Every day men prove their worth by working hard, sacrificing for their families, and serving their communities.

I'm not a particularly macho fellow, but a few years ago I took up home remodeling. I enjoy slicing boards and driving nails, partly because it feels manlier to me than sitting at a computer all day (my regular job). My desire to fill my masculinity bank results in a nicer home for my family. When a project is finished, I invite over my friends, who praise my carpentry skills (*ka-ching, ka-ching*). Even writers and artists like me have a masculinity bank to fill, and we must find clever ways to prove our manhood because we lack a macho persona and profession.

Masculinity banks experience withdrawals as well. If a man fails in manly endeavors, he loses a few coins. If he's exposed as a coward, a cheat, or a cheapskate, he loses a few more.

But nothing empties a masculinity bank faster than womanly behavior. Doing something "girlie" is like pulling the stopper out of the bank and dropping coins down a sewer. That's why those beer ads resonated—the sight of a man emasculating himself by wearing a woman's skirt or skintight jeans is so weird and repulsive that men react on a gut level. The campaign transmits a powerful promise: "Drink our beer and your masculinity bank is safe."

o o o

Unfortunately for the church, many men see churchgoing as womanly behavior. It's the polar opposite of the risky, dangerous image they try to project. Men don't go to church for the same reason they refuse to carry anything that resembles a purse—it's not something guys do. Imagine this scene one Wednesday night after a long, hot day on the construction site:

BILL. Hey, where you guys going after work?

DEAN. I'm going out for a beer.

JEREMY. I've got tickets to the ball game.

BILL. How about you, Sam?

SAM. I'm going to Wednesday night church service.

ALL. [*Silence*]

Men, do you feel that one in your gut? Dean and Jeremy are planning an evening of manly behavior. But Sam will be doing something *real* men don't do—going to church, and on a weeknight.

This is one reason many Christian men hide their faith from other men. They're not ashamed of Christ; they're ashamed of feminization.

I must confess, I have been in Sam's position. Instead of being straightforward about my plans to attend a religious gathering, I've learned to tell the truth in vague, man-acceptable terms, such as, "I'm getting together with some friends," or, "I'm just spending some time with the family." How clever of me.

Churchgoing men employ a variety of strategies to guard their coins. If a man goes to church for purely cultural reasons but there's clearly no commitment to Christ, the masculinity bank remains intact. I call this the Mafia strategy. These men, like Mafia dons, attend church to preserve cultural tradition or to keep women happy. But are they true followers of Jesus? *Fuhgeddaboudit.* They sit in church with arms folded, shielding their hearts from the love of God. I suspect many of these men realize they are hypocrites, but they don't care: their precious manhood is intact.

o o o

Do men really associate church with femininity? One Saturday, I polled men outside a sportsmen's show in Anchorage, Alaska. Ninety-five guys responded to this query: "I'm going to read a list of twelve places where people gather. Please tell me whether these places have a more feminine feel or a more masculine feel."

Here's what the guys said:

	Masculine	Feminine	Undecided
Football Stadium	83	1	11
Baby Shower	0	95	0
Flower Shop	4	74	17
Gun Show	85	1	9
Elementary School	1	54	40
Church Service	*11*	*30*	*54*
Hospital	14	27	54
Bar	59	2	34
Fishing Boat	76	0	19
Shopping Mall	1	67	27
Sunday School	*3*	*50*	*42*
Office Building	26	19	50

As you can see, church services and Sunday school were perceived as feminine more often than masculine. Only eleven men perceived church as masculine, and just three perceived Sunday school that way. It's not a shutout, like baby showers (which no one saw as manly). But it's clear that lots of men pick up the scent of a woman in our houses of worship.

Why does this matter? Because a typical man won't do something he believes is feminine. It costs his masculinity bank too many coins. This is why men don't hang out at baby showers, flower shops, craft bazaars, or froufrou boutiques. *What will the guys think?*

Doggone it. Can't men just get over this obsession with manliness? No, they can't. You might as well ask a woman to get over her maternal instincts. The need to be manly is universal and buried deep—the product of a thousand generations of conditioning. Manliness is not something a man does; it's a vital part of who he is.

o   o   o

How did we get here? How did a religion founded by a man and his twelve male followers gain the reputation as a "ladies' club" in the minds of men? It started with the division of Jesus into two men. That's the subject of our next chapter.

Discussion questions for this chapter are available free at www.churchformen.com/guides.

Chapter 6

THE TWO JESUSES

IT'S A CRISP NOVEMBER MORNING AS WORSHIPPERS FILE INTO THE ornate stone church at the corner of First and Prescott. The congregation is celebrating 150 years of ministry in the same location. The new minister, the Reverend Sheila Crocker-Jimenez, steps into the pulpit and surveys the crowd. About 125 worshippers are scattered throughout a sanctuary that once held 700. There's a lot of gray hair in the audience.

Rev. Crocker-Jimenez begins her sermon with a reading from Matthew 11 (KJV). "Come unto me, all ye that labour and are heavy laden, and I will give you rest," she says, her words echoing off the stained glass and sandstone walls. Over the next twenty-five minutes, she weaves a beautiful tapestry of Christ's love and comfort. She wraps up her homily with a great promise of Scripture: "John tells us that God *is* love. Think about that. If God is completely love, then there is no part of him that is *not* love. So don't approach him in fear; approach him in faith, because he loves you and accepts you just as you are. Come unto him, and he *will* give you rest. Amen."

Meanwhile, six blocks north, at the corner of Seventh and Prescott, another congregation of 125 souls is worshipping in a nondescript building with stucco walls and royal purple pews. Lace curtains flutter lazily as a cool breeze pushes through the open windows. The pastor (called Brother Raymond by his flock) has also chosen Matthew 11 for his text. But his sermon sounds and feels strikingly different from the one being preached down the street.

"The Bible says that the *fear* of the Lord is the beginning of all understanding!" Raymond shouts, as the congregation offers up a smattering of *amens*. Raymond wipes his brow with a freshly pressed handkerchief. He picks up his black leather King James Bible and begins to read, "And thou, Capernaum, which art exalted unto heaven, shalt be brought down to hell." Raymond stops, allowing the word *hell* to hang in the air. "For if the mighty works, which have been done in thee, had been done in Sodom, it would have remained until this day. But I say unto you, That it shall be more tolerable for the land of Sodom in the day of judgment, than for thee" (vv. 23–24). Raymond looks up at the crowd. "Folks, we're living in a modern-day Capernaum. Be ready; the hour of judgment is almost at hand!"

o o o

Two pastors, representing the same faith. Reading from the same chapter of the same Bible. In fact, their chosen Scripture passages are next-door neighbors, residing just five verses apart. Both declarations flowed from the mouth of the same man—Jesus of Nazareth.

Yet these sermons—and the holy words that inspired them—could hardly be more different. It almost sounds as if these two ministers serve different gods.

There are two Jesuses afoot in the world today. They are both based on a partial understanding of Christ. I call one the Lamb of God; the other, the Lion of Judah. Sheila follows the Lamb, while Raymond follows the Lion.

The Lamb of God (a.k.a. the Prince of Peace) is the famous one. He's the one who wept over Jerusalem, welcomed children to his side, and showered compassion on the suffering. He taught us to *judge not* and to *turn the other cheek*. Lamb-Jesus is the Christ of popular culture, media pundits, and politicians, who point to his compassion when justifying increases in government spending.

The Lamb of God is extremely popular in mainline churches.

He is also an honored guest at seeker-friendly congregations and is becoming a mainstay in so-called emerging churches. He's the consensus pick on websites, blogs, and discussion boards. People who never read the Bible (but who think they know a lot about God) endorse this Jesus. When pollsters ask average folks, "What is Jesus like?" their answers usually describe Lamb-Jesus.

The Lion of Judah (a.k.a. the King of kings) is the one you don't hear much about. He's the one who seemed to revel in conflict. He's the Christ who declared, "I did not come to bring peace but a sword"[1] So wild was this Jesus that he used physical violence to advance his kingdom. If our Lord pulled this stunt today he'd be the hottest story on cable news. Let's go live to the courtroom, where the plaintiff's attorney has just begun his opening remarks:

> My client was operating a legitimate business in the temple courts. One afternoon the defendant, Jesus of Nazareth, fashioned a whip and assaulted my client. He also destroyed my client's property and scattered his earnings across the ground. We are suing for punitive and compensatory damages, and we recommend a long prison sentence to remove this public menace from the streets.

While the Lamb of God exhibits a Zen-like calm, the Lion of Judah seems to fly into a rage at the drop of a sandal. He's constantly rebuking a friend, offending a Pharisee, or pronouncing doom on a city.[2] He ignores the plea of a desperate woman because she's not Jewish, and then he insults her people by calling them "dogs."[3] If Christ uttered these words today, he'd be tossed out of the church as a racist and a sexist.

The two Jesuses are ripping denominations apart. The leaders in liberal mainline churches have run headlong after the Lamb of God, while many of their members still cling to the Lion of Judah.

Lion and Lamb are duking it out on the Internet. I just saw a heated discussion on a Christian website titled "Are Competition and Christ Compatible?" The responses were split: many described competitiveness as "the way God made us," while others saw our lust for victory as a by-product of the fall. Brandon O'Brien spoke for the latter camp when he wrote in *Christianity Today*, "Humanity in the image of Christ is not aggressive and combative, it is humble and poor (Phil. 2:5ff). We are most like Christ not when we win a fight, but when we suffer for righteousness' sake (Eph. 5:1-2; 1 Thess. 1:6; 2:14)."[4]

The confusion extends to your local Christian bookstore. While many pastors beg their flocks to behave like the Lamb of God, Christian authors hawk books about the Lion of Judah. Religious books encourage us to live a life of *Risk*, to become a *Radical*, and to live *Wild at Heart*.[5] It's easy for authors to endorse kamikaze Christianity—they don't have to stick around and clean up the damage the Lion of Judah always leaves in his wake.

The Lion of Judah was very popular in fundamentalist churches as recently as a few years ago, but even here his sun is setting. It's no wonder why. He doesn't seem to be a very good Christian.

Let's measure the Lion against the famous "fruit of the Spirit" passage in Galatians 5:22–23. The apostle Paul identifies "love, joy, peace, patience, kindness, goodness, faithfulness, gentleness and self-control" (NIV) as the marks of a Spirit-filled believer. But if this is the definitive test of Christian character, Lion-Jesus flunks on almost every count. Christ had a volcanic temper and regularly expressed *impatience* with his disciples.[6] He didn't show much *peace, gentleness*, or *self-control* while swinging that whip and overturning tables.[7] He hurled stinging insults at both friend and foe, words that were hardly *loving* or *kind*.[8] *Joy* eluded him as he neared the cross.

Here's something few people realize: Lion-Jesus isn't the exception; he's the rule. See for yourself: grab a cheap paperback New Testament. Take a pink highlighter and mark all the passages where Jesus is tender, loving, and kind. Then take a blue highlighter and mark the verses where he's tough, challenging, and wild. You'll be shocked at how much lion you find.

Nevertheless, most churches have locked the Lion of Judah away in the attic like some crazy uncle. They rarely speak of him and only allow their members to imitate him in Three Blessed Exceptions:

1. In evangelical churches, you may be a lion when fighting for souls, or "witnessing" to others.
2. In mainline churches, you may be a lion when battling poverty, racism, and oppression.
3. In charismatic churches, you may be a lion when battling demonic powers (spiritual warfare).

Other than the Three Blessed Exceptions, Christians are always expected to be gentle as lambs. The public believes this. The media believes this. And increasingly, the church believes it too. People grudgingly acknowledge that Jesus had a few lionlike moments, but believe Christ is, at his core, a lamb. (As evidence, recall the Venus/Mars quiz I gave you in chapter 1.)

The church likes the Lamb of God because he's more acceptable in modern society. Today's ministers want to distance themselves from the judgmental, pulpit-pounding religion many people grew up with. As a result, modern pastors consistently preach the Lamb of God and emphasize Christ's grace, gentleness, and humility.

Ministers also like the Lamb because he's such a good role model to the parishioners. Lambs are much easier to control than lions. They're docile and easy to lead. What pastor would want a church full of lions, overturning the missions bake sale table and warning the new members' class of impending doom?

o o o

Most religions are based on the teachings of their long-dead founders, but Christianity is rooted in the founder himself. Christians are first and foremost imitators of a living man named Jesus. Christianity flows from an understanding of his essential nature. In other words, *who Jesus is* forms the foundation of our faith and holds as much weight as what Christ did, said, or taught.

This understanding of who Jesus is becomes a filter through which we interpret what we read in the Bible. When we come across a passage where Jesus is being disagreeable, rude, or aggressive, we do not take this as our example. We say to ourselves, "Jesus' aggression in this passage is a metaphor for how we are to combat injustice in our world." We see temple-clearing Jesus as a Lamb with PMS—having his monthly meltdown—and dismissing it with, "Oh, he's not usually like this."

When the Lion of Judah shows up in church, we do not recognize him. Instead, we condemn and declaw him. People who speak the truth too boldly are stifled because they might hurt someone's feelings. Leaders who make bold moves are accused of being power hungry. Efforts to make the church more efficient or effective are tabled in the name of harmony. Churches that set specific goals and measure achievement are looked down upon for being "too focused on numbers." A number of pastors even refuse to speak some of the Lion's favorite words, such as *sin*, *repent*, and *hell*.

o o o

Because churchgoers believe Jesus is a Lamb, they expect every experience in church will be a pleasant one. When it's not, they get upset. Tim Stafford has noticed a growing epidemic of persons who feel wounded by the church.[9] Today's Christians abandon their congregations over the smallest hurt or disappointment. They seem surprised or indignant when another believer points out sin in their lives—as if this is something Christ would never do.

I recently spoke to a pastor who refuses to admit into church membership couples living together outside of marriage. He gently shows the couple what the Bible says about extramarital sex and challenges them to conform to that standard. And for his efforts this pastor has received angry messages from parents, friends, and even the couples themselves, calling him narrow-minded and judgmental. "Three generations of our family have attended this church," one woman screeched over the phone, "and *you* are refusing membership to my daughter because of her living arrangements? How dare you! Who are you to judge my daughter?"

People are so convinced of God's meekness they no longer fear his wrath. (Who fears a raging lamb?) God is not seen as a judge who holds us accountable for our actions; he is a protector who watches over us. He's no longer a disciplining father; he is a doting grandfather.

o   o   o

By creating and worshipping a half-Jesus, Christians have unwittingly made the gospel less compelling to my half of the human race. The more Christians follow this half-Jesus, the more feminized Christianity becomes. Church preaching and teaching, music, décor, language, ministries, outreach, and mission increasingly reflect the gentle side of God—and only his gentle side. As God becomes softer, so does our theology. Judgment disappears, replaced by universal-ism, a doctrine that deeply offends men's innate sense of justice. (The thought that Adolf Hitler might be enjoying heaven is nauseating to all but the most feminized of men.)

The Lion of Judah is like canned spinach. He's sometimes slimy, unpleasant, and hard to swallow, but he builds muscle—especially in men. His insane courage, bold truth-telling, and severe absolutism ignites a flame in my heart. I love the Lamb of God, but I'm intimi-dated by the Lion of Judah. That creates the tension that makes Jesus so fascinating to men.

I'm not suggesting a return to old-fashioned fire-and-brimstone preaching. It is God's kindness—not his judgment—that leads to repentance.[10] There are still many people who erroneously believe God is an angry grouch sitting in the sky, counting our sins and sending misfortune to punish us. A severe Jesus who is all judgment holds little appeal for women or men.

But a Christ who is all grace cannot stir the masculine soul. Deep down, men long for a harsh affection—the love of a coach who yells at his players to get every ounce of effort; the love of a drill sergeant who pushes his recruits to the limits of human endur-ance; the love of a teacher who demands the impossible from his students. As Western society feminizes, it's getting harder for men to find this kind of love. The Lion of Judah offers harsh father-love in abundance—yet he's becoming an endangered species in the modern church.

It's funny. Ask men what the church should be and you'll hear words like *loving, nonjudgmental, freedom to do what you want, caring for the poor,* and *compassionate.* Yet the churches that specialize in these things (the mainline) are practically bereft of men.

Men may say they want the Lamb of God, but something in their hearts yearns for the Lion of Judah. It is no coincidence that C. S. Lewis chose a lion as the Christ-figure in his Chronicles of Narnia series. Had he chosen a lamb to portray Aslan, no boy would have read his books.

The final section of this book is a plan to release the Lion of Judah back into his natural habitat—the local church. Yes, there will be turmoil. When lions roam free, a bit of chaos is inevitable. But it is the only way to recapture the hearts of men—and to fulfill the church's mission on earth.

Discussion questions for this chapter are available free at www.churchformen.com/guides.

PART 2

CHURCH
CULTURE VS.
MAN CULTURE

Up to this point I've been pretty general in explaining why men resist church. Now we get down to specifics.

Remember the story of the straw that broke the camel's back? For the next eight chapters we'll sift through the pile of straws that are squeezing the masculine spirit out of our churches. Individually, these straws are trifles, but together they form a heavy burden that is crushing men's hearts.

Before we dig into this pile of straws, here's my top-ten list of excuses men give for not wanting to go to church:

10. I don't have time.
9. Church just doesn't work for me.
8. It's boring.
7. It's irrelevant to my life.
6. I don't like the pastor.
5. I don't want to talk about it.

4. It's too long.
3. They ask for money too much.
2. It's for wimps.

(*drum roll, please*)
The number one reason men give for not going to church is the perennial favorite:

1. There are too many hypocrites there.

Do these excuses address the real reasons men don't go to church? Not really. Women face the same challenges but still make church a priority. If you want to get past the excuses to discover the real barriers, you must ask why: Why do men think it's too long? Why do men find it boring and irrelevant? Why do men think there are too many hypocrites? And here's the big one: why are these attitudes so common in men but less often found in women?

Chapter 7

VICTORIA'S SECRET . . .
WHEN WE LOST THE MEN

MOST PEOPLE ASSUME CHRISTIANITY'S GENDER GAP IS SOMETHING new. Back in the old days, men used to be more religious, right?

Wrong. Men have been underrepresented in the church for at least seven hundred years, according to Dr. Leon Podles, a Catholic scholar of religion and author of the book *The Church Impotent: The Feminization of Christianity*.[1]

Men began to withdraw from church life during the thirteenth century. Catholicism shifted its adoration from a male deity (Jesus Christ) to a female one (the Virgin Mary). A doctrine of weakness and dependency replaced the church's historic emphasis on struggle and self-sacrifice. As the ranks of priests grew, clergymen assumed the role of practitioners of the faith, while laymen became utterly passive, unable even to feed themselves the Lord's Supper.

The Protestant Reformation captured the hearts of men—for a while. Religious men settled the New World, but their unction did not always guarantee their presence in the pews. New England churches whose rolls go back to the 1600s show the majority of their members were always women.[2]

During the Victorian era, Christianity's relatively small gender gap became a yawning chasm. Economic and societal changes rocked Western society. Definitions of manhood and religion changed in tandem. Men began leaving the church en masse; women remained.

Before 1800, in the Western world it was simply assumed that every respectable man was some form of Christian. Well-educated men went to church. Religion, government, and higher education formed a triad that maintained the civil order.

But during the nineteenth century, male intellectuals began publicly rejecting religion as superstition or myth. Atheists "came out of the closet" and admitted they did not believe in God. A new term was coined to describe those who believed in God's existence but not his involvement in human affairs: *agnostic*. Many of the West's great universities, founded as religious institutions, secularized during this period. Religion morphed from a public, civic identity into a personal, private choice.

Once society's leading men began abandoning church, it wasn't long before the rank and file followed. The great evangelist Charles Finney wrote in the 1830s: "Women composed the great majority of members in all churches." Even in the post–Civil War Bible Belt, one observer wrote, "The altars of our churches are pitiably devoid of young men," and, "There has scarce been a religious young man here in years."[3]

a surplus of women

softening of preaching,
music, and theology

explosion of female-
oriented ministries

softening of male
clergy

While upper-class males were rejecting Christianity for reasons of intellect, workingmen were forced out of the church by economic pressures. The Industrial Revolution completely changed how the laboring classes worked and lived. Instead of staying home on the farm, men toiled long hours at mines, mills, and factories, some of which operated on Sundays. Other men had to leave town to find work, far from home and familiar parish.

Who remained to fill the pews? Women, children, and elderly men. The able-bodied male all but disappeared from Sunday worship. This population shift created a vicious circle that changed the very nature of Christianity—and launched the church model we have today.

SOFTENING OF PREACHING, WORSHIP, AND THEOLOGY

In the previous chapter, I introduced the two Jesuses. Pre-Victorian Christians were much more familiar with God as the Lion of Judah. You can see this influence in the title of the best-known sermon of the eighteenth century: "Sinners in the Hands of an Angry God."[4]

But Victorian ministers learned that an angry God did not connect with audiences that ran up to 75 percent female. So they replaced him with the Lamb of God, a warm, comforting deity who matched the sensibilities of the predominantly female congregation. "Jesus, Lover of My Soul" was a perfect companion and protector for women whose husbands had little time for them. This softening of God has been going on for about two hundred years and shows no signs of stopping.

During the late 1800s, Victorians began decorating their sanctuaries according to a domestic motif, rejecting the austere, mirthless facilities of their Puritan forebears. Victorians brought carpets, draperies, padded chairs, flower arrangements, quilts, and ribbons into the church. Stained glass made a comeback, restoring a burst of color to the worship space.

Nineteenth-century revivals introduced emotionalism to the church. Weekly services remained sober affairs, but tent revivals provided an outlet for exuberance in worship. In 1906, the Azusa

Street Revival introduced modern Pentecostalism to the church. Suddenly the excitement of a revival was available every week. "Spirit-filled" worship stressed informality, personal expression, displays of emotion, and the individual touch of God. Considered an oddity a century ago, this highly expressive brand of Christianity is quickly becoming the dominant model in the West today, particularly in developing nations.

SOFTENING OF MALE CLERGY

Just as tall men have an advantage in the game of basketball, gentle and sensitive men suddenly had an advantage in the pastorate. In the 1800s, seminaries began to fill up with less-than-manly men, precisely because their softness made them so lovable to the matrons who held the levers of power within the church. Ann Douglas writes, "It seems highly likely that, in a period when religion was more and more the province of women, many of the young men drawn to the church were seen to be deeply attached and even similar to the women they knew best, namely their mothers."[5]

During the Victorian era, men and women were consigned to strict gender roles, but pastors were something in between, a special class of men who were allowed to exercise feminine gifts. Pastors moved in feminine circles, preaching to women, counseling women, drinking tea and eating cakes with women. The sallow, sickly pastor was a common character in literature of the day. One turn-of-the-century writer lamented, "Too often sissy fellows have paraded themselves as representatives of Christianity's crowning work and characterization, while the men of full-blood and ambition have quietly dropped out from such company."[6]

EXPLOSION OF FEMALE-ORIENTED MINISTRIES

Victorian pastors may have been sissy, but they weren't stupid. With their flocks predominantly female, they knew their careers depended on their ability to keep women happy and engaged.

Ministries targeted at subgroups (such as women's ministry, children's ministry, youth ministry) were rare before 1800. But Victorian clergymen discovered women needed something to do—particularly well-to-do women whose husbands were becoming wealthy capitalists. Churches enthusiastically sopped up that spare time with innovative programs that met women's needs. Ladies' teas, sewing circles, temperance unions, and women's missionary societies all made their debuts in the Victorian church.

Before the Victorian era, children's ministry as we know it today did not exist. There were no special programs for the little ones; they simply attended services with their parents. But in the 1800s an innovative pastor looked out on his flock and saw the future: Squirmy children + lonely grandmothers = opportunity.

Thus were born the first pullout programs for the young: Sunday school and the church nursery. These ministries solved two problems: pastors could preach without interruption, and lonesome grandmothers (whose children had moved to faraway locales) were given a weekly appointment with tots. Children's ministry was an instant smash hit. No other program has done more to cement women's commitment to church.

As the twentieth century dawned, the local church was the primary gathering place for respectable American women. It became the locus of female influence and power. Women locked arms with their pastors to oppose male pleasures such as drinking, gambling, cursing, and whoring. They pressed mayors to pass vice laws and shutter red-light districts. Their political alliance in the United States reached its zenith in 1919–20 with the passage of the Eighteenth and Nineteenth Amendments, which made alcohol illegal and gave women the right to vote.

As the twentieth century rolled on, church ministries further specialized, reaching out to smaller and smaller subgroups. Singles. Alcoholics. Junior high kids. Immigrants. Soldiers. The homeless. And who provided the "manpower" for this ever-expanding roster of ministries? Women.

o o o

After World War II, Americans began leaving the denominations of their birth and started "church shopping." This new breed of religious consumer often chose a church based on the ministry programs it offered, particularly children's and youth ministries. By the 1960s these ministry programs were no longer optional: a church had to offer them, or shoppers—excuse me; parishioners—would flee to the competition.

Now the church was utterly dependent on women. Congregations could not grow without an extensive roster of ministry programs. And ministry programs could not function without women. Therefore, any church that hoped to grow had to keep women happy and volunteering. The Victorians established the symbiotic relationship between women and volunteerism that serves as the engine of the modern ministry machine.

Think of the local church as a ship. The captain is likely to be male, but his officers and crew will be primarily female. So if the skipper wants the ship to run smoothly, he must be able to please and motivate women. Clergymen learn early in their careers that *if mama ain't happy, ain't nobody happy*. Should the captain run afoul of certain powerful women, he'll have a mutiny on his hands. The ministry engines will sputter and die. So pastors work overtime to make women feel loved and needed. Of course, this brings more women into the church. And the circle is complete.

o   o   o

The Victorian-era church had gained such a reputation as a "woman's thing" that any man who remained involved with it risked being thought of as effeminate or henpecked. As a result, men stopped mentioning their faith around other men. It became unmanly for men to discuss religion at all—except to criticize it.

This reputation clings to Christianity today. A lot of men feel that church is for women, weirdoes, and wimps. They think to themselves, *Christianity is for little old ladies of both sexes.*

Chapter 8

THE CHRISTIAN-
INDUSTRIAL COMPLEX

GILLETTE HAS INTRODUCED THE WORLD'S FIRST FIVE-BLADE DIS-
posable razor.

Correction—Gillette has introduced two of these super razors.
One is called Venus Embrace. The other, Fusion ProGlide.

Venus Embrace is sold under the slogan, "Reveal the Goddess
in You." It comes in four colors: Spa Breeze, Tropical, Oceana, and
Malibu. It's curved and soft to the touch. The Venus Embrace has its
own website, done up in white, green, and aqua. It features an image
of a beautiful woman with a child clinging to her slender, hairless legs.

Gillette's other five-blade wonder is named Fusion ProGlide.
It comes in one style: chrome on black. This razor is angular and
resembles a weapon an alien might use on *Star Wars*. Gillette's website touts the ProGlide's "breakthrough blade technology," "advanced
low-resistance coating," and an "improved blade suspension system."
The ProGlide website is mostly black with splashes of luminescent
blue. There are no images of children on this site.

Want to know the truth about these two products? They offer
exactly the same shave. The part that does the cutting—the five-
blade phalanx—is identical. But you'd never know that by looking
at the advertising.

In case you haven't figured it out, the Venus Embrace is for women, while the Fusion ProGlide is for men. So why would Gillette go to all the trouble and expense to produce two versions of the same product? Years ago, executives learned they can sell more razors at a higher price when they launch a separate model targeted at each gender.

o   o   o

Feminists often criticize advertisers as stereotype-driven sexists for placing babies, butterflies, and blossoms in their female-targeted ads. But as a thirty-year veteran of the media business, I can tell you exactly why those girlie images are there—*because they work*. Stereotypically feminine imagery really does encourage women to open their wallets.

Here is the politically incorrect truth: there are measurable, verifiable differences in the way men and women perceive the world. Whether these differences are hard-wired or socially programmed is beside the point. They exist. Men and women respond favorably to different things. They're attracted to different things. They're repelled by different things.

While there are always individuals who don't fit the pattern, the genders as a whole are quite predictable. Gillette executives know that certain women will be turned off by Venus Embrace's prissy marketing campaign. They're also aware that some men will dismiss the Fusion ProGlide as macho posturing at its worst. But these businessmen don't care. They know men will buy a razor that looks like a weapon, and women will buy a razor that's soft and curved. When they build their sales pitches around the tastes of the majority in each gender, they sell more razors.

Now, what has this got to do with church? You're probably thinking I'm about to recommend that churches follow the lead of advertisers: study men, deploy lots of masculine imagery in church, and present the gospel in a Fusion ProGlide–inspired package.

Nope. There's no need to do any of this. Because it's already happened—in reverse.

o o o

The vast majority of Christian culture and messaging is already targeted at the wants and desires of women. Modern Christianity is being packaged like a Venus Embrace. And we don't even realize it. Here's why.

In the previous chapter we saw how women came to dominate church life during the Victorian era. Industrialization expanded the ranks of women who had disposable time and income. Nineteenth-century pastors devised a host of ministry programs to put that capital (human and financial) to work.

In twentieth-century America, businessmen had a similar revelation. They saw under those steeples a huge, predominantly female market. So they created products and services to capture a slice of that market.

The result is what I call the Christian-industrial complex, a network of manufacturers, distributors, retailers, broadcasters, and content producers (that's me)—all hoping to make a buck off the religious market.

I'm not impugning the motives of anyone working in the complex. Most of us earn a lot less than we could in other industries. We do it for love of Christ. Nonetheless, profit does figure into the equation. Projects get the green light based on their ability to reach the most people. And in the case of the Christian market, "most people" means women.

The Christian-industrial complex keeps pumping out products for women. Christians of both genders use these products and absorb the ideas therein. Soon, everyone is looking at the Christian faith through a feminine lens. The weight of all this female-targeted religious material is beginning to warp the faith it's supposedly describing. The more Christian products we consume, the more we come to perceive our faith in feminine terms.

This is why Christians are so shocked when the Lion of Judah raises his head in church—he seems so out of place. The deluge of female-targeted products has changed the way Christians perceive

Jesus, church, and worship. They've bent our customs, our vocabulary, our décor, and even our theology in the feminine direction.

The feminization of Christian culture is not a conspiracy—it's simply the result of an institution and industry finding its market. When Christian manufacturers target women, they make more money. When religious broadcasters target women, they get bigger audiences. And when churches target women, they get more volunteers. It's a simple numbers game.

Retailing

In every Christian bookstore in America, the women's section is bigger than the men's section—usually three to four times bigger. Savvy booksellers know women buy about 75 percent of Christian products, so they work hard to create an atmosphere of femininity. The moment a man walks into a religious shop, he knows he's out of his element. Susan Faludi describes her visit to a Christian bookstore this way:

> The "men's" section was consigned to a back shelf. . . . [It was] hopelessly outnumbered and outflanked by the pink devotional pamphlets and rose-adorned spiritual guides that lined the other shelves, frilly Bible covers and lambs-and-chicks crib ruffles that jammed the cabinets, flower-festooned jewelry and smiley-faced Jesus figurines that blanketed the display cases, out-of-focus portraits of serene homemakers sipping tea and sniffing flowers that covered the walls, and uplifting sugary music that emanated from floral jewel boxes, windup infant mobiles, and music-box-bearing stuffed animals, generating a cacophonous cross talk of treacle.[1]

A look at the Christian Booksellers Association (CBA) top one hundred Christian books shows "six titles directed to the special needs of men and 21 titles to the special needs of women. This latter category, which ranges from *Hugs for Mom* to *Bad Girls of the Bible*, reflects the fact that most buyers of CBA books are women."[2] In fact, the CBA magazine does not have a men's interest category. When Pat Morley, one of America's leading men's ministers, approached CBA about starting one, he was turned down.[3]

Not only do women read most of the Christian books; they write most of them as well. Although many of the blockbuster titles are still written by men, there are far more females writing for the religious market. At the last Christian writers' conference I attended, my gender was outnumbered 13 to 1.

What do all these devoted women want? To be loved.

Here's a sad truth: there are millions of love-starved Christian women. They're either single (can't find a godly man) or they're trapped in loveless marriages. And unlike their secular sisters, they've got few options for catharsis. They can't have an affair. Female porn is off-limits. Even steamy romance novels or sexy rags like *Redbook* and *Cosmopolitan* are frowned upon in the church.

So the Christian-industrial complex has stepped in to fulfill these women's need for a purer kind of love. Christian romance is one of the fastest-growing categories in fiction. These romances are mostly harmless fantasy—stories of heroic prairie women who find handsome, strong men who plow fields by day and pray with their wives at night.

But not everything is so chaste. Christian self-help books are prodding women to become lusty—toward Jesus. Many famous authors vigorously encourage women to imagine Jesus as their personal lover. One tells her readers to "develop an affair with the one and only Lover who will truly satisfy your innermost desires: Jesus Christ."[4] A well-known Christian author says to his female readers, "At times, Jesus will be more of a husband to you than the man of flesh that you married. And while your husband may wonderfully meet many of your needs, only the Bridegroom can and will meet all your needs."[5] Another offers this breathless description of God's love: "This Someone entered your world and revealed to you that He is your true Husband. Then He dressed you in a wedding gown whiter than the whitest linen. You felt virginal again. And alive! He kissed you with grace and vowed never to leave you or forsake you. And you longed to go and be with Him."[6]

Some would argue there's no harm mixing in a little *eros* with the *agape* when it comes to women. But Jesus-is-my-boyfriend imagery is beginning to migrate to men as well. These days, it's fairly common for pastors to describe a devout male as being "totally in love with Jesus." I've heard more than one men's minister imploring a crowd of guys to "fall deeply in love with the Savior." I just saw a book that invites Christian men to "get close enough to reach up and kiss His [Jesus'] face."[7]

Such imagery is unbiblical, unappealing, and some would say unhealthy for Christian men. We'll discuss the romancing of Jesus in much greater detail in chapter 12.

Broadcasting

Women are more likely to watch Christian television than are men. Barna Research found that women are the primary users of all forms of Christian media. Women support televangelists with their prayers and checks. The older the woman, the more likely she is to watch.[8]

Christian talk radio is dominated by female-oriented content. Three of the most popular syndicated Christian radio talk shows in the US are *Focus on the Family, Family Life*, and *Family Talk*. Do you see a pattern? Who's more likely to listen to a show about family issues: men or women?

Women are more likely to listen to their local Christian radio station. Radio listeners in general are an exact replica of the population: 51.7 percent female, 48.3 percent male. But Christian AC radio (the format playing on most contemporary Christian music stations today) draws an audience that's 63 percent female and 37 percent male. Christian stations garner, on average, 21 percent more female listeners than do mainstream stations.[9] I do not know of a Christian radio station anywhere on earth that draws as many male as female listeners.

K-Love, America's largest syndicated Christian music radio network, targets its programming at eighteen- to forty-five-year-old females. Two-thirds of K-Love listeners are women. Its sister service, the upbeat AirOne, also draws twice as many gals as guys. Christian radio stations around the nation report up to three-quarters of their core listeners are female.

As the name implies, K-Love's playlist is heavy on love songs— tunes that express our love for God and his love for us. Like most Christian music stations, K-Love shies away from anything edgy or raucous. Its on-air slogans are "Positive and encouraging" and "Safe for the whole family." It's not unusual for K-Love to play a heart-tugging testimonial from a listener whose life was "deeply touched" by something she heard on the station.

The K-Love disc jockeys have created a mythical average listener, whom they call Kathy. She is a mother in her midthirties with two kids, a minivan, and a mortgage. Kathy is very busy, driving her kids to soccer practice, piano lessons, and youth group. As she drives, she listens to K-Love. Kathy's name comes up frequently during staff meetings, and the DJs make sure their on-air antics won't upset or offend her sensibilities.

So how is this strategy working? In an era of radio consolidation and retreat, K-Love continues to grow. During the 2000s, the network more than doubled its number of affiliates. K-Love may now be the largest female-oriented broadcast network in the United States.

o o o

A century ago, Christianity was feminizing from within. Today, forces outside the church are accelerating this trend. Money is driving it.

Every year a multimillion-dollar torrent of products and services floods the Christian market, targeting the spare time and disposable income of devout women. These products gush into our churches, small groups, and homes, slowly eroding the masculine foundations of the faith. Christianity is taking on the characteristics of the Venus Embrace—soft, curved, and convenient. It still cuts— but ever so gently.

So what's the answer? Start wrapping the gospel in a manly package?

Here's a better idea: Why not remove the girlie packaging the Christian-industrial complex has wrapped around the Christian faith? Lift up Christ as he is, and he will draw all men.[10]

Chapter 9

MEN AND CONTEMPORARY WORSHIP

APRIL 2, 1961, WAS MY FIRST SUNDAY IN CHURCH. IT WAS EASTER.
I was less than a month old, so I don't remember much. My baptismal certificate records the name of the church: Redeemer Lutheran in Green Bay, Wisconsin.

That Sunday, Mom and Dad carried me into a well-lit sanctuary. Sunlight poured in through stained-glass windows, dappling the pews in a fiesta of color. The room was full of religious symbolism, including several ornate crosses. We were handed a mimeographed "order of worship" bulletin as we entered. Men wore suits and ties; women wore skirts, hats, and gloves. The pews were packed, and the service began with a candle-lighting processional. Then an energetic man in a choir robe instructed us, "Turn in your hymnals to number 159." He pivoted and faced an identically robed choir, which led the congregation in song, backed by a Wurlitzer organ. The songs were familiar, and the entire congregation sang robustly, except for me, because I was asleep. The adults alternately stood and sat, as instructed by the choirmaster. The only electronic item in the room was a microphone affixed to the pulpit.

Fast-forward exactly fifty years—to April 2, 2011. I attended the Saturday night service at a contemporary megachurch. It was a very different experience.

We sat in a darkened, windowless room, devoid of religious imagery. Both men and women wore casual clothing—T-shirts, jeans, and even shorts. There was not a single necktie or skirt in the building. Nor was there a bulletin or an "order of worship"—nothing to suggest that there was even a plan for the evening's proceedings. The service seemed to begin organically, as a soft-spoken man in designer jeans and thick, plastic glasses stepped forward and began strumming a Taylor six-string guitar. He was backed by a rock band and a sophisticated sound system, computer-controlled lighting, and smoke machines. The room was nearly empty at first, but it gradually filled during the sixteen-minute worship set. (No one told us to stand, but we did anyway.) Multiple video cameras captured the event and magnified it on two large video screens. Lyrics were superimposed over the video rock show, but almost no one in the crowd was singing them.

o   o   o

For centuries Protestant worship was fairly static. But toward the end of the twentieth century, worship changed—not just in style, but in function. The old worship was formal, corporate, and emotionless. The new worship is informal, individualistic, and touchy-feely. The old worship was about coming together to extol God; the new worship is about coming together to experience God. The target of worship has fallen half a meter—from the head to the heart.

Most people assume the transition to new worship has been a good thing. Young people seem to like it. Growing churches all offer it. It's simply assumed that new churches will offer praise and worship (P&W) instead of traditional hymnody.

But is the new worship a good thing for men? Before we can answer that question, we must understand why Christian music changed so completely at the end of the twentieth century—and how that change is affecting the way Christians worship God.

o   o   o

During the late 1960s, young hippies began turning to Jesus. They went to church but found the music to be a real bummer. Old-fashioned hymns didn't connect with kids who had grown up listening to the Rolling Stones, Creedence Clearwater, the Beatles, and Janis Joplin.

So these young Jesus Freaks began composing songs to their liking, and formed rock bands to perform them. Early 1970s acts such as Daniel Amos, Randy Stonehill, Phil Keaggy, and Sweet Comfort Band launched a new genre known simply as Jesus Music. It later came to be called Contemporary Christian Music (CCM).

The combination of rock music and the gospel was a combustible mix in the early 1970s. Many believers had decided that rock and roll was of the devil after watching Elvis gyrate on the *Ed Sullivan Show* in 1956. During the 1960s, rock music was seen as the gateway to sex, drugs, and immorality of every kind.

So early Jesus Music bands struggled to get by. Churches barred them from using their facilities. Christian radio stations refused to spin their records. Concert promoters wouldn't book them. Yet the bands soldiered on, playing whatever gigs they could find, often for free, depending on "love offerings" to put enough gas in the tank to reach the next city.

Things began looking up in the late '70s. Christian bands became more polished. They started filling larger venues. A few churches began inviting them in. Secular rock stations began playing CCM on Sunday mornings. Hit albums sold in the tens of thousands. Some acts even made a little money.

In 1978, a seventeen-year old schoolgirl released her first CCM album. Within a decade, Amy Grant changed the course of sacred music—and in the process, altered the way Christians worship God.

Amy Grant was a record-sales juggernaut. Her *Age to Age* was the first CCM album to go platinum. She later crossed over into secular pop, greatly expanding her reach. She has won multiple awards, has sold more than thirty million records, and was even hired by a major national retailer to endorse its products.

Amy Grant proved that Christian musicians could have mainstream appeal—and earn buckets of money. Grant's success attracted millions of investment dollars to the Christian music industry. CCM radio stations began popping up all over the United States. More Christian acts crossed over into secular music—increasing their potential for evangelism—and earnings.

This influx of cash allowed Christian concerts to become just as sophisticated as secular ones—with advanced lighting, sets, effects, video, and sound. By 1995, the only difference between sacred and secular concerts was the obligatory talk about Jesus—and the lack of pot smoking in the audience.

CCM concerts and stadium events not only changed Christian music—they began changing people's perception of what worship can and should be. Young believers became accustomed to worshipping in darkened rooms, under stage lighting, with a rock band in the lead. Young adults came to accept large video screens, special effects, and even smoke machines as a part of worship. And they experienced something previous generations of worshippers never had—*the worship high*—that euphoric feeling one gets from singing with a vast multitude of highly committed believers (who paid to get in).

Naturally, these young concertgoers began to ask, "Why can't my congregation worship like this every week?" Thus began a decades-long intergenerational conflict, which came to be known as the "worship wars."

On the one side stood traditionalists, who clung to their hymnals, organs, and four-part harmonies. Their songs were old-fashioned, complex, and theologically rich. On the other side stood the contemporaries, with their guitars, drums, and keyboards. Their songs were modern, simple, and easy to memorize. They invented a new genre of church music that has come to be known as "praise and worship" (P&W).

During the '70s most churches simply ignored the growing influence of praise and worship. But by the late 1980s, congregations that did not offer P&W were losing young people—particularly the committed young believers who attended CCM concerts and knew that worship music didn't have to come from the plume of Franz Joseph Haydn.

By 2010, the worship wars were all but over—and worship won. Today, praise songs are sung in almost every church on earth. Guitars, drums, and electronic keyboards are ubiquitous in all but the most traditional churches. Hymns are still sung, but in many contemporary churches they're treated as treasured relics—rolled out once in a while when a music set needs a bit of gravitas.

Amy Grant just wanted to sing songs about Jesus, but her success set in motion a chain of events that has altered the way Protestants worship God. Not only has it changed the style of music, but our very worship spaces are morphing into rock concert halls. New churches are building dark, windowless auditoriums with lighting trusses and an elevated stage. Music pulsates from stacked speakers. Video cameras capture a rock show and project it back to us on big screens. Worship leaders dress exactly like their Christian music heroes. Even traditional churches are playing catch-up, by hanging projection systems in the sanctuary, and by investing in sophisticated sound and lighting gear.

o   o   o

And so we come to the big question: Is the new worship good for men? The answer is yes and no.

On the positive side, praise and worship greatly simplified sacred singing, placing men who can't read music on an equal footing with the classically trained. The simple, repetitive lyrics of early praise songs were also a boon to men who had spent years tripping over Elizabethan lyrics such as, "Here I raise mine Ebenezer, hither by thy help I'm come . . ."

P&W is also set to a modern beat and uses the same instruments men play and listen to for pleasure—guitar, bass, drums, and keyboard. Projecting the lyrics on the big screen makes it easier for men (and women) to participate, eliminating the need to flip through a hymnal. Worship leaders can now transition seamlessly from one song to the next, without having to call out a page number and wait for the congregation to catch up.

The informal nature of modern worship is a strong plus for men. Most guys never did like getting dressed up for church. They like being able to wear shorts and drink coffee during the service. Worshipping in the dark gives them some anonymity, a big plus for many guys. Men like to watch TV—so the addition of big screens to the worship space is probably a good thing.

So the new worship offers a lot for men. But overall, I believe P&W has harmed men's worship more than it has helped. This is hard for me to write, since I have been a fan of CCM and the new worship since the '70s. But the evidence seems to indicate that, while P&W is very appealing to some men, it's a turnoff for many more.

Before P&W, Christians sang hymns *about* God. But P&W songs are mostly sung *to* God. The difference may seem subtle, yet it completely changes how worshippers relate to the Almighty. P&W introduced a familiarity and intimacy with God that's absent in many hymns.

With hymns, God is *out there*. He's big. Powerful. Dangerous. He's a leader.

With P&W, God is *at my side*. He's close. Intimate. Safe. He's a lover.

Most people assume this shift to greater intimacy in worship has been a good thing. On many levels, it has been. But it ignores a deep need in men:

Modern Christianity has taken a decisive turn toward feminine religion, which is typically interested in the immanent and the incarnational, and finding God in the small things, the everyday, and the mundane. . . . As liberal religion stresses increasingly the immanent and "horizontal" dimension of faith to the exclusion of the transcendent and "vertical" reality, it inadvertently ignores the voracious appetite of man for the Great, a Wholly Other, and the Eternal.[1]

Although hymns are old-fashioned, they still have what it takes to stir the male soul. They march forward in 4/4 time. They extol God's power, grandeur, and might. The great hymns summon men to the battlefield—but many of today's P&W songs seem to be summoning men to the bedroom. Some contain man-love imagery that's plainly uncomfortable for men.

Picture two male hunters sitting in a duck blind, shotguns resting across their laps. One hunter decides to express his affection for the other, using the words of a popular praise song. He turns to his friend and says, "Hey, buddy . . .

> Your love is extravagant
> Your friendship, it is intimate
> I feel I'm moving to the rhythm of Your grace
> Your fragrance is intoxicating in this secret place."[2]

Readers, I cannot imagine saying these words to another man—especially one carrying a loaded shotgun.

Lovey-dovey praise songs force a man to express his affection to God using words he would *never, ever, ever* say to another guy. Even a guy he loves. Even a guy named Jesus.

The Bible never describes our love for God in such erotic terms. The men of Scripture loved God, but they were never *desperate for him* or *in love with him*. Men are looking for a male leader—not a male lover.

Not every P&W song is so amorous. Some songs get the lyrics right—but are set to slow, dreamy music. This reflects women's tastes. Market research shows that men like robust, fast-paced music with a driving beat. For example, album-oriented rock, known for its blaring guitars and bone-crushing percussion, draws an audience that's 69 percent male. But soft adult contemporary, known for its tender love songs, attracts 67 percent female listeners.[3]

Today's worship leaders are under pressure to re-create the *worship high* every Sunday. This is nearly impossible, since a roomful of casual churchgoers is not nearly as passionate about music as a concert audience that paid a steep admission fee to get in. Nonetheless, we judge worship leaders on their ability to help the crowd "enter into worship" (translation: respond emotionally to the music).

A top-tier worship leader knows how to do this. He starts the set with a potboiler. Then he slowly brings the tempo down to a simmer. The lights dim. He repeats a verse. He repeats a verse. He repeats a verse. Then, with tinkling piano in the background, he shares a heart-tugging story. The crowd is under his spell. He finishes his set with a breathy, eye-closing, microphone-squeezing number that tries to wring every last drop of passion from the audience. The song builds to a mighty climax that summons a burst of energy from the assembly. After a round of applause, the satisfied worshippers return to their seats, emotionally and physically spent, bathed in the afterglow of heartfelt worship, ready to cuddle up with a message from the pastor.

As I visit various churches, one constant is the *softness* many worship leaders bring to their ministry. Softness in their personalities, their vocabulary, and the way they express themselves. Spiky hair, skinny jeans, fake plastic glasses, and flat-toed shoes are now standard attire among worship leaders. What causes this?

In the Old Testament, priests led worship, so you had a diversity of personality types in leadership. But today's worship leaders have one thing in common: they are all musicians. That means the bulk of our worship pastors are right-brained, artistic types. They may be feminizing worship just by being themselves.

o o o

The transition from old worship to new worship has proceeded with amazing speed. And few people recognize the hidden hand behind this revolution: the Christian music industry and its lust for profit.

Fifty years ago, worshippers sang songs handed down by long-dead composers. But today, our sacred music is being served to us by an industry that wants us to buy what we're singing.

This financial incentive may be driving one of the hottest trends in worship today—congregations that never repeat a song. A number of churches in the US sing all new tunes every week—and they never sing them again. Once and done. Pastor Chuck Swindoll says,

"I have been to church services, and you have too, where the only people who knew the songs were the band. I'm not edified. I'm just watching a show. And they're not interested in teaching me the songs either. They just sing louder to make up for the fact that no one else is singing."[4]

Swindoll is right on. I visit churches all over the US. About half the time I don't know a single song the band plays. And I'm not alone. I look around the room and almost no one seems to know them. Not even the young people. Guys stand in silence with their hands in their pockets, while a few wives and girlfriends try to sing along. Getting men to sing songs they know is hard enough—good luck getting them to sing songs they've never heard.

But record companies smile. They don't want us singing yesterday's tunes—they want to expose us to new stuff on Sunday, so we might buy it on Monday. Some praise bands don't even wait that long. I recently attended a contemporary worship service at which the band performed all original songs—and then offered them for sale on CD after church. The merger of rock concert and worship is complete. I hope God is pleased.

Meanwhile, the gatekeepers in the Christian music industry serve up a steady stream of female-friendly products. Ever wonder why there are so few praise songs with a masculine flavor? Why male artists croon to Jesus in the overwrought style of Michael Bolton? Why Christian songs with an edge get so little airplay? The Christian music industry knows its audience—lonely women who long for a lover, and cautious mothers who want to protect their children. Meeting their expectations keeps the cash registers ringing.

Now, hold on. I'm not suggesting some massive kickback scheme where music companies are paying off worship leaders. But the industry has its ways. They send bands on tour. They sponsor mega worship conferences with big-name singers. Church musicians flock to these events and experience the worship high. And they say to themselves, "Whoa, that was awesome! I've got to bring that experience home." They play the songs. They dim the lights. They pump up the crowd. They pluck at the heartstrings.

o o o

We have a conundrum. Men flock to churches with contemporary worship. But they don't seem to like it all that much. Many seem to endure the music to get to the sermon. Some go so far as to show up late to church—or stand in the lobby—in order to avoid the singing altogether. I call these men *praise skippers*.

Women have outsung men in church for a hundred years (just check the gender distribution in the choir loft), but in P&W congregations the men have pretty much stopped singing at all. Worship leaders seem unaware. Bright stage lights keep them from seeing past the first couple of rows, and in-ear monitors prevent them from hearing the astonishing lack of baritone voices.

Men are doers, and singing was one of the things Christians used to *do* together in church. It was a chance to get involved. Now, with congregational singing going away, and Communion no longer a weekly ordinance, there's only one avenue left for men to participate in the service—the offering. Is this really the message we want to send to men? *Sit back, relax, and enjoy the show. And don't forget to give us money.*

o o o

There's nothing wrong with professionalism and quality in church music. The problem isn't the rock band, or the lights, or the smoke machine. I'm not suggesting that contemporary churches go back to hymns and choir robes.

But men need songs they can sing. Songs they're familiar with. Set in the right key. With singable lyrics that extol the power of God. Without the moaning and manipulation. The new worship can be tremendously powerful, if it's done with men in mind.

Discussion questions for this chapter are available free at www.churchformen.com/guides.

Chapter 10

Twelve Things Men Fear About Church

Though they probably wouldn't admit it, many men are afraid to go to church. That's right, afraid.

We've already exposed one of men's biggest fears in chapter 5: *church forces a man to violate multiple man laws.* We now examine a dozen other fears, to help you appreciate the panic that grips a man's heart when you ask, "Would you like to go to church?"

1. "I'll Hate Church, Like When I Was a Kid"

Men often have a harder time forgetting a traumatic experience than women do. This is because of a difference in brain structure.[1] So if men were traumatized in church as children, they're more likely than women to retain those fears as adults.

Since the majority of US men were raised in church (at least for a time), they bear some childhood memories of it. And if those memories are bad, they may feel distressed every time they enter a house of worship. The sight of stained glass or the smell of musty hymnals can summon vivid, painful memories years later.

It doesn't take horrific abuse to create negative childhood memories. Some boys were just bored out of their minds—and they're loath to repeat the experience as adults. As a little boy, I remember sitting through lengthy church services, wearing a stiff, collared shirt and choking necktie, my feet squeezed into uncomfortable patent leather shoes. At the ripe old age of seven, I made myself a promise: *Once I'm grown up, I'm never going to do this again.* God found me as a teen, but most men who utter this vow keep it the rest of their lives.

One reason contemporary churches seem to do a better job reaching men is their rejection of *old-time religion.* Their modern style doesn't stir up painful memories of childhood. Of course, some men had a wonderfully positive church upbringing, and these are the ones you're most likely to find in the pews of traditional churches.

2. "I'll Lose Control"

A man's greatest fear is *powerlessness,* whereas a woman most fears *loneliness.* According to Sam Keene, a man's worst nightmare is a loss of control—to become disabled and dependent on others. A woman's worst fear is a loss of relationships—to be abandoned, left alone, and unloved.[2]

When Sam and Sally go to church, they hear a message like this: "You need to give control of your life to God and enter into a personal relationship with the One who will never leave you or forsake you." For Sam to embrace this message, he would have to face his deepest fear—loss of control. But for Sally, the gospel means she'll never have to face her greatest fear—she'll never be unloved. Who's getting the more attractive offer?

There are many other controls a man must give up when going to church. For instance, he loses control of his time. If a church service is long, boring, irrelevant, or weird, he's stuck. Out of politeness, people rarely get up and leave. So a man feels trapped. *I gave up my weekend for this?* he thinks.

Men fear being singled out for attention at church. Most guys would rather come and go anonymously, but some churches ask visitors to stand and be recognized. Men usually hate this attention.

3. "I'll Get Stuck with Some Weirdo"

According to an article in *Christianity Today*, who is America's most famous evangelical? It's not a televangelist, politico, or megachurch pastor. It's Ned Flanders, the Bible-quoting, teetotaling neighbor on the animated TV series *The Simpsons*.[3] Ned's a stereotypical Jesus nut who's cheery, straitlaced, and . . . nerdy. Flanders is the nicest guy you could ever meet, and if you think he's weird, that's just *okely-dokely* with him.

There's a certain peculiarity that comes from following closely after God (think John the Baptist), but some Christians have taken weird to a new level (think Nehru-jacketed televangelist). We've all known Christians who have gotten excited about the Lord and gone completely off the end of the pier.

Some men fear if they were to become religious, they might end up like Flanders. Or they'll find themselves in some secret assembly of wide-eyed religious fanatics. ("Excuse me; could you pass the Kool-Aid, please?")

Men also fear that a life of faith spells the end of fun. Giving up your weekends to sing songs and listen to sermons doesn't sound appealing to your average guy. Christians also have a reputation as straitlaced prudes who don't drink, don't smoke, don't dance, don't play cards, don't go to movies, and don't associate with those who do. Most men would rather attend a dull party than a great Bible study.

4. "Is He Gay?"

I remember the good old days when preachers used to have affairs with women.

Today's headlines shriek: LOCAL PASTOR ACCUSED OF IN-APPROPRIATELY TOUCHING MEN. MINISTER DEFROCKED FOR SECRET GAY RELATIONSHIP. PRIEST ACCUSED OF MOLESTING BOYS. Then there are headlines like these: CHURCH DEBATES GAY MARRIAGE. DENOMINATION ELEVATES GAY BISHOP. The media has worked overtime associating the words *church* and *gay*, to the point that men are starting to think the church is chock-full of closeted Liberaces.

They're not far from the truth. Homosexuality is widespread in many churches today. Experts estimate that anywhere from 15 to 50 percent of Catholic priests in the US are gay.[4] If you're a black man looking for a homosexual hookup, just go to church. So says J. L. King, a bisexual who claims to have found multiple male sex partners in African-American congregations.[5] Michael Stevens, an African-American pastor from North Carolina, says that in many congregations it's a not-so-quiet secret among parishioners that their minister is involved in secret homosexual relationships—even as he thunders against the practice from the pulpit.[6]

These gay undercurrents can cause a man to keep the church at arm's length. The fear of an unwanted advance makes guys think twice before joining a men's small group or meeting with a guy from the church for coffee. It suppresses attendance at the annual men's retreat. Some men are afraid to send their sons to church camps or to allow the boy to be mentored by another man.

5. "If I Become a Christian, I'll Become Soft"

In the 1800s, Charles Spurgeon said, "There has got abroad a notion, somehow, that if you become a Christian you must sink your manliness and turn milksop." Men have long feared that if they turn to Christ, they will soften, lose their killer instinct, and fall behind their competitors. They'll become wimps. Jesse Ventura, a former governor, pro wrestler, and Navy SEAL, spoke for millions of men when he said, "Organized religion is a sham and a crutch for weak-minded people who need strength in numbers."[7]

This judgment may be untrue or unfair, but the reputation clings to Christianity like a leech. It's curious—a devout Muslim is considered *manlier* among his peers, whereas a devout Christian is often seen as a wuss.

6. "Church Is Tough on Single Guys"

Single guys ages eighteen to thirty-five are the demographic least likely to attend church—and we don't make it easy on them. I have a number of single, churchgoing buddies who describe the subtle pressure they feel to settle down and get married. One friend of mine (a single man in his thirties) says the matrons of the congregation are constantly asking if he's got a girlfriend. He's even had one offer to be his matchmaker. And since there are so few eligible bachelors in his church, going to a singles' meeting feels like "walking into a roomful of bees with honey smeared on your face."

Becoming a Christian also means that one must bring his sexual life into line with scriptural standards. Thanks to their higher levels of testosterone, young men generally have a higher sex drive than young women. They fear that if they were to become Christ-followers, they would not be able to contain the fire that burns within.

7. "Christians Don't Get Much Sex"

Since the Victorian era, the church has been associated with extreme prudery when it comes to sexual matters. The image of Christians is: they don't talk about sex, they don't like sex, and they probably don't get much sex. Today's unchurched men regard biblical prohibitions against premarital sex as outdated, and priestly celibacy seems just plain bizarre.

There's no way to be delicate about this, so I'll just say it. Some men are reluctant to go to church because it says to the world, "I'm not getting much sex." A churchgoing single guy says to the world, "I'm not getting any." In some circles a single man who's voluntarily celibate is believed to be sexually impotent or gay.

This is a huge subconscious hurdle for a lot of men. Even men who aren't sleeping around are loath to put a sign on their heads that says, "I've been sexually tamed." Church affiliation implies that you are not performing as a man. Plus, Christian men mustn't engage in locker-room boasting, a primary form of male communication.

Believe it or not, churchgoing can actually inflame lust in a man's heart. It's a weekly appointment with throngs of women who look their best. Contemporary churches attract lots of young women—many of whom dress provocatively, to say the least. The exposed cleavage and tight-fitting garments that made spring break famous are now appearing at a worship service near you.

I talked to one man who had to change churches because of this issue. A particularly well-built young woman would regularly go forward to wave a flag during worship. She often wore an embarrassingly tight tank top and jiggled sensually during the praise music. "I know this woman just wanted to praise her Savior, but her dancing was very suggestive," he said. "All she lacked was a brass pole." I suggested he mortify his flesh by joining a mainline congregation. Lust is no problem in a church where the average woman is pushing sixty.

8. "Church Is Full of Hypocrites"

What's the most common excuse you'll hear from men who avoid church? *There are too many hypocrites.* Men expect perfection from the church, and they feel entitled to point out its shortcomings. Why is hypocrisy such a problem for men but not for women?

Perhaps the answer lies on the cover of *Family Circle.* At least four times a year, this women's magazine features a cover shot of some scrumptious-looking dessert oozing with chocolate, cream, and nuts. And printed just above this eight-hundred-calorie delicacy is a headline that says: LOSE 10 LBS. IN 3 WEEKS. There is an obvious contradiction between the headline and the photo. But women don't see hypocrisy; they see hope.

Pastor Mark Gungor believes men avoid church because they know that if they hear the Word, they will have to become doers of the Word.[8] They know their lives don't measure up to God's standards, so they skip church out of a sense of integrity. They wouldn't want to become hypocrites themselves.

9. "All They Want Is My Money"

Men are expected to earn a good living and accumulate possessions. Having the right stuff is important to men. It's one way they prove their manhood. A big, bad truck, a trophy home, a nice boat. Like it or not, men size each other up by what they own. (Churchgoing guys are no exception; believe me.)

This need underlies men's most common complaint about church: "All they want is my money." The church wants it both ways: a man is supposed to drop 10 percent in the plate, but he gets in trouble for working too many hours. Giving not only affects his bank balance but also crimps his ability to prove himself through the accumulation of possessions.

Once a man starts giving, he learns that those who give, receive. Still, this lesson can be harder for a man to learn because society expects him to be flush.

10. "I'M JEALOUS"

Country songwriter Hayes Carll penned this lyric:

> *She left me for Jesus,*
> *And that just ain't fair*
> *She says that he's perfect*
> *How could I compare?*[9]

When a woman falls in love with Jesus, her boyfriend or husband may panic. Linda Davis writes, "All he knows is that she's in love with someone else, and he is jealous. Instead of remaining the first priority in her life . . . he has suddenly been demoted to number two after God."[10] How is a man supposed to compete with someone he can't even see?

Today's American man typically has just one friend: his wife. When Jesus enters the picture, she's got a new best friend. Men feel rejected, so they fight back the only way they know how: by refusing to have anything to do with church. *Take that, Jesus!* It's a normal male response to a rival.

Some women fall hard for Jesus; others for the church—or the pastor. Sabrina Black recalls a time when she returned from church to her husband's withering stare. "If I want anything done around here, all I need to do is call the church and let your pastor tell you because you do what the pastor says to do," he said. "When the pastor says he needs somebody, you come running. When the pastor says there is a committee or a project, you show up. If I ask you to do something, you are too busy."[11]

Sons also notice when Mom is gone all the time, feeding her savior complex. Boys think, *Church is something that takes Mother away.* Sons can become just as resentful as husbands, but they may not feel entitled to speak up.

11. "I'm Being Held to an Impossible Standard"

Thanks to women's magazines, TV shows, and Dr. Phil, married men are held to a pretty high standard these days. But married Christian men are expected to be superhusbands. Kevin Leman writes, "Not only are [Christian] men supposed to attend morning Bible studies, but they're also supposed to get home in time for dinner, spend time alone with each child, date their wives once a week, and earn enough money so that their wives can stay home with their young children. This is a heavy load, and some Christian men start to resent it."[12]

In church, the unspoken assumption is that men are broken and in need of repair. Nancy Wray Gegoire writes, "I've often noticed that sermons on Mother's Day tend to gush over moms, while on Father's Day they tell dads to shape up."[13] No wonder men skulk away like dogs that have been kicked one time too many.

Almost every religious book for men is focused on a single target: making better husbands and fathers. Men's ministry meetings pound the same drum. *Be a better husband and father. Keep your promises. If your wife isn't happy, you're to blame.* Family harmony received scant attention from Jesus. How did it become the primary focus of men's ministry? After a while a man begins to wonder, *Is the church in league with my wife?*

12. "I'm Afraid of Heaven"

Let's end this chapter on a lighter note. Popular notions of heaven strike fear in men's hearts. What man wants to spend eternity wearing a white robe, floating on clouds, plucking a harp? Men fear heaven because it sounds so dull. No challenge. No uncertainty. No fun. In heaven there's nothing to do.

Excuse me; there is one thing to do: sing. As a youngster, John Ortberg sang in the youth choir under the direction of Mrs. Olson. He said, "When she became frustrated with the boys, she'd clap her hands and say, 'You children better start singing, because when we get to heaven, that's what we'll be doing.' For an eleven-year-old boy, the thought of ten billion years under the enthusiastic direction of Mrs. Olson was not my idea of eternal bliss."[14]

An eternity singing in the choir. Contrast this with Mormon heaven, where faithful men spend the afterlife making celestial babies. Or consider Muslim heaven, where martyrs enjoy the everlasting ministrations of seventy-two virgins. Guys, which sounds better to you: eternal singing or eternal sex? Is it any wonder why Mormonism and Islam are growing so rapidly and are so popular with males?

Chapter 11

THE STARS VS. THE SCRUBS

AT 6 FOOT 8 AND 235 POUNDS (2 M, 107 KG), MARK RANDALL was a physical presence on the basketball court. Randall led the Kansas Jayhawks to the NCAA championship game and was a first-round pick by the Chicago Bulls in 1991. His rookie season, the Bulls won the NBA title—but no thanks to Mark Randall. Over the course of the entire '91 season, Randall was on the court just 67 minutes and scored a measly 26 points.

A men's NBA team has fifteen players. But only eight or nine play during a typical game. These players are known as the *stars*. The rest of the players are nicknamed *scrubs*. The scrubs are also known as *benchwarmers*, because that is what they do night after night. Their only hope of seeing action is if one of the stars is forced to leave the game due to injury, cold shooting, or foul trouble.

Mark Randall was a scrub. He was a very talented, well-paid basketball player, but he lacked the full complement of skills the stars brought to the game.

It's tough being a scrub. Scrubs work just as hard, exercise just as much, and suit up for every game, but they rarely get to play because somebody else is a little bit better than they are. I'm sure Mark Randall battled discouragement as he watched his teammates flying to the hoop. He must have felt useless.

When it comes to churchgoing, most women are potential stars, while most men are potential scrubs. Why? Natural ability. As we saw in chapter 1, the average woman possesses the skills that allow her to participate fully in the game. But the average man lacks the churchgoing skills that come naturally to many women.

I'm not talking about spirituality. I'm referring to the mundane, practical abilities that allow a person to function at a high level in a gathering of Christians. Women are just better at "doing church" than men are, because the rules of church favor women. The natural abilities that help a person become a star in church can be summed up in three words: *verbal, studious,* and *sensitive.*

A star churchgoer must be *verbal:*

- Enjoys listening to spoken lessons and sermons.
- Is sociable and good at small talk.
- Possesses verbal fluency to pray aloud and comment in small groups.

A star churchgoer must be *studious:*

- Reads well.
- Loves to study.
- Is able to find texts in books, analyze these texts, and form decisive conclusions.
- Possesses teaching ability.

A star churchgoer must be *sensitive:*

- Relationship oriented.
- Nurturing with children.
- Introspective.
- Loves music and singing.
- Emotionally perceptive.

Multiple studies, surveys, and polls have shown that the average woman is more likely than the average man to fit the star profile. Here's how it breaks down.

A Star Has Verbal Skills

Anne and Bill Moir wrote, "This basic difference between men and women is fundamental and is confirmed by an extraordinarily wide body of research: women are generally more verbal, men are more spatial. She is good with words, he is good with things."[1]

The female brain is wired for verbal expression and comprehension. Reading is a relatively complex task that draws on both sides of the brain at once—and women have superior links between the hemispheres. This may explain why males are diagnosed with reading disorders such as dyslexia at four times the rate of females.[2] Fifty-five percent of women read literary works for pleasure; just 37 percent of men do so.[3]

Now think about church. From the moment you walk in the doors, it's a Niagara Falls of verbal stimuli: Bible readings, study guides, spoken lessons, responsive readings, and song lyrics, not to mention spoken prayers and after-service conversation.

The centerpiece of Protestant worship is the sermon—a nonstop gusher of words. Here's what I want to know: just who decided that the lecture-style sermon was the best way to teach people about Jesus? According to many studies, a long, uninterrupted monologue is the least effective way to teach people anything.[4] And who has the hardest time learning from a lecture? Men.

A Star Is Studious

In the past thirty years, women have zoomed ahead of men academically. About three-quarters of girls graduate from high school, while only about two-thirds of boys do. Women attend college at higher rates than men, where they compose 56 percent of the undergraduate student population and 59 percent of graduate students.[5]

Much of the modern Christian life is built on an academic model: we offer Sunday *school*, Bible *study*, vacation Bible *school*, and Christian *education*. About half the square footage in our churches is devoted to classroom space. Small groups usually gather around a book.

A STAR IS SENSITIVE

You don't need a study to confirm that women are often more sensitive than men. The average female is more concerned with relationships, more child-oriented, and more emotionally perceptive than the typical male.

Concerning music: Doesn't it seem as though girls are more likely than boys to receive formal music training as children? I recently attended my daughter's piano recital, where I heard twenty-six girls and five boys perform. Women's early exposure to music helps them appreciate our second most popular church pastime: singing.

Of course, these are all generalities. Certain men can outtalk, outstudy, and outempathize any woman. Some men are virtuoso musicians, gifted teachers, or obsessive bookworms. But considering the genders as a whole, the gifts and experiences that make one an ideal churchgoer are more commonly found among the fairer sex.

STARS FIT THE VOLUNTEER PROFILE

It's not just her natural abilities that allow the female to soar above the male in church. Most volunteer opportunities involve roles that have historically belonged to women. The average US congregation of eighty-four members needs volunteers in seven main areas:

- Child care
- Teaching
- Music
- Cooking
- Gatherings (weddings, funerals, etc.)
- Committee work
- Ushering

Given this list of opportunities, where do most men end up? "Here's your bulletin, ma'am. Can I help you find a seat?"

Are there brothers willing to work in the nursery, cook for

potlucks, and don a choir robe? Of course there are, and God bless them. But these have been women's roles for centuries, and many men feel ill qualified or even embarrassed in them (more about this in chapter 23).

o   o   o

There's a reason our pews are filled with women. There are more females in the population whose skills and experiences match the culture of the church. In short, most women are potential stars.

But guys? Most are potential scrubs. They know it too. They lack the natural abilities to excel in church. So they focus their time and energy in venues where they can be stars. The workplace. The golf course. The fishing boat.

Joe is a furnace repairman. He's a star at installing and maintaining heating and cooling systems. He's good with his hands and can repair almost anything. He's also a skilled hunter and fisherman.

But get him into a church, and suddenly he's a scrub. He lacks the skills one needs to be a good churchgoer. His abilities (fixing things, troubleshooting, and project management) are almost useless in church. He's not very good at study, chitchat, or child care. He's reluctant to pray aloud, to attend Bible studies, or to volunteer because he's afraid he won't do it right. Joe believes in God, but church leaves him feeling like a dope.

What's worse, the man who runs the church is a star. The worship leader is a star. The guy who teaches adult Sunday school is a star. That fellow on the front row who's raising his hands and crying is a star.

As these men shine, Joe feels even more like a scrub.

Stars do all the planning in the church, so they program based on the needs and expectations of other stars. They like lots of singing, study, and socializing. So that's what the church offers. Stars never even consider the needs of the scrubs, because they can't relate to a person who may not find God through singing, study, and socializing.

The church's traditional approach to scrubs is to assume they can be made into stars. The thinking goes: *All Joe needs is the infilling of the Holy Spirit and suddenly he'll like to read aloud, study books, sing robustly, and develop emotional sensitivity.* When this doesn't happen, everyone assumes Joe must not really have a personal relationship with Jesus. And Joe wonders himself why he doesn't derive much joy from church activities Christians are supposed to like.

Let's go back to our basketball example. Here's why Mark Randall got so little playing time during the Bulls' championship season: he had a teammate named Michael Jordan—arguably the greatest man ever to play the game. Jordan could function at a very high level within the basketball system, so he got all the minutes—while Mark Randall "rode the pine."

But after three consecutive championships, Jordan walked away from basketball and tried baseball. Jordan placed himself in a new athletic system that required a different set of skills. Suddenly, the world's greatest athlete was mediocre. He gave it his all, but no amount of determination, coaching, or training was enough. Michael Jordan simply didn't have the skills to become a great baseball player.

So His Airness returned to the NBA and promptly won three more championships. Jordan found contentment once again in his area of competence.

Michael Jordan + basketball = high competence

Michael Jordan + baseball = low competence

Men + church = low competence

A lot of talented men have realized they are incompetent within the church system. The rules and expectations are stacked against them. No amount of determination, coaching, or training is going to change this. Neither will prayer, preaching, or the Holy Spirit. So they quit. Or they sit on the bench, watching the women and soft men score all the points.

Men + work and hobbies = high competence

Just like Michael Jordan, men find their greatest joy in their area of competence. Put another way: men devote themselves to things they're good at. This is why men pour themselves into their work and hobbies: these are oases of male competence. But for most men, the church is not.

Of course, this begs the question: Why are the rules of the church system so skewed toward verbal, sensitive, and studious people?

Which leads to a second question: Is this truly what church was meant to be?

Which opens a whole box of questions: What if the church system were different? What if the rules and expectations of church were altered to allow average Joes to score more points? Again, it's not about changing the gospel or Jesus or doctrines or beliefs. It's about creating a culture where both men and women know they can get in the game, score some points, and help the team win.

Chapter 12

CHECK YOUR TESTOSTERONE
AT THE DOOR

NOT EVERY MAN HAS A SPECIFIC REASON FOR HATING TO GO TO church. Some just feel a general unease with it. Rod says, "Church just doesn't work for me." Lance is a little more specific: "The style of worship is not compelling to me. It's just the feel of the whole thing. Emotionally, it doesn't connect with me." Conrad is blunt: "Every Sunday I feel like I'm supposed to check my testosterone at the door." Why do men feel manhood and Christianity are incompatible? Here are some specifics.

CHRISTIANS USE FEMININE LANGUAGE,
THEMES, AND TERMINOLOGY

Remember our Venus/Mars quiz in chapter 1? People are more comfortable thinking of Jesus as having the gifts that come naturally to a woman. Therefore, Christians tend to use feminine vocabulary when describing their faith. References to sharing, communication, relationships, support, nurturing, feelings, and community are sprinkled throughout the conversation of Christians—both men and women. Woody Davis found that Christian men emphasize themes and endorse messages that unchurched people—both men and women—regard as womanly. In other words, Christian men talk and think like women, at least in the eyes of the unchurched.[1]

Liberal churches have removed masculine pronouns from hymns, liturgy, and even Scripture, in an effort to make women feel more comfortable in church. (Note to liberals: it's working.) Some Bible translations are expunging masculine references (*sons of God* is now *children of God*) but retaining feminine ones (*bride of Christ*). Some politically correct pastors refuse to use male pronouns at all, even when referring to God. Some have even neutered the Trinity. Father, Son, and Holy Spirit no longer authorize baptisms; that power now rests with the androgynous Creator, Redeemer, and Sanctifier.

Conservatives use man-repellent terminology as well. For example, in the Baptist universe you have two kinds of people: the saved and the lost. Men hate to be both. Men can't stand being lost—that's why they don't ask for directions. And the only thing worse than being lost is being saved. Throughout the literature of a thousand cultures, men are always the saviors, while women are the ones being saved. Today's Hollywood blockbusters still follow this ancient formula—Spider-Man rescues Mary Jane, not the other way around. It goes against the cultural grain for a man to assume the feminine role.

Another term from the feminine side is *sharing*. Christians often say things like, "Steve, would you please share with us what the Lord has placed on your heart?" Regular men don't talk this way. It sounds too much like kindergarten. Imagine a gang member saying to one of his brothers, "Blade, would you please share with us how you jacked that Mercedes?"

Jesus spoke constantly of the kingdom of God.[2] Men are kingdom builders. They think hierarchically. But many churches have replaced the masculine term *kingdom of God* with the more feminine *family of God*. Jesus never uttered this phrase. Nevertheless, it's become a favorite of pastors worldwide. "We're a loving family of God, here to worship Jesus," they cry. "We're so happy you've chosen to join our family this morning." They prefer to speak of church as a "family" because the word resonates with the feminine heart. (I've devoted chapter 13 to this issue.)

THE LANGUAGE OF RELATIONSHIP AND ROMANCE

Religion has a bad rap in our culture. The very word *religion* conjures images of people practicing empty rituals, going through pointless motions, devoid of power and bereft of love. Postmoderns tend to see religion as old-fashioned, oppressive, and false.

So when a person has a life-changing encounter with Christ, he needs a new way to speak of his faith. He needs terminology that tells everyone he's not simply practicing the old, dead religion of the past. Twentieth-century evangelicals coined two phrases that attempt to separate living faith from dead piety. Both have become very popular, and unfortunately, both are somewhat repellent to men.

The first of these terms is *a personal relationship with Jesus Christ.* It's almost impossible to attend an evangelical worship service these days without hearing this phrase spoken at least once.

Curious. While a number of Bible passages imply a relationship between God and man, the term "personal relationship with Jesus" never appears in the Scriptures. Nor are individuals commanded to "enter into a relationship with God."

Yet, despite its extrabiblical roots, *personal relationship with Jesus Christ* has become the number one term evangelicals use to describe the Christian walk. Why? Because it frames the gospel in terms of a woman's deepest desire—a personal relationship with a man who loves her unconditionally. It's imagery that delights women—and baffles men.

Nowadays it's not enough to have a personal relationship with Jesus; many of today's top speakers encourage men to have a *passionate* relationship with him. They invite men to rest in his arms, look up into his eyes, and experience a warm, gooey feeling for him. Speaking as a man, the idea of having a passionate relationship with another guy is just plain gross.

The second phrase popular with preachers and authors is *intimacy with God.* The term is spreading like a virus through the church, communicated by men with advanced degrees who write religious books. Here's an example I read just this week: "Through Jesus God reveals that he loves us passionately and longs for an intimate relationship with us."[3]

So what's the problem? God loves us. What's the harm in using this quasi-romantic language to describe what we have with him?

Think of the mental gymnastics that must take place in a man's mind as he pictures himself becoming passionate with Jesus—kissing him, staring into his eyes, or lying in his arms. If you don't detect homosexual undertones in this imagery, you're not looking very hard.

Just like *personal relationship with Jesus*, the Scriptures never use the term *intimacy with God*. And lest you think I'm dirty minded, whenever the words *passionate* or *intimate* appear in the Bible, they always refer to sex or lust between humans.

When a man loves another man, he uses the language of respect. "Hey Joe, you're a stand-up guy. I admire you." Men do not speak of passionate, intimate, or even personal relationships with their leaders or male friends. Can you imagine a couple of bikers having this conversation?

> **ROCCO**. Hey, Spike, let's go for a ride in the desert so we
>   can develop a passionate relationship.
> **SPIKE**. Sure, Rocco. I'd like to enjoy some intimacy
>   with you.

One time I was sitting in a men's ministry training session. A middle-aged man stood up and said, "I have a passion for men, particularly young men." I thought, *Hm. I know a counselor who can help you with that.*

Conservative churches may oppose homosexuality, but their imagery is sending another message entirely. The more they describe Christianity as a passionate, intimate relationship, the more nervous men become.

One more thing on relationships: men really do need to have a relationship with God. Religion without relationship is bondage. The problem is the word *relationship*. It's not a term men use in conversation, except when describing a male-female couple.

(Phone ringing)

RON. Hey Bruce, it's Ron from the church. How you
    doing?
BRUCE. Fine, Ron. What's up?
RON. Hey Bruce, can we have a personal relationship?
BRUCE. [*click*]

In chapter 19, we'll examine better options for describing the
Christian faith—phrases Christ himself used to draw men into his
service.

WOMANLY DÉCOR

You may think that men don't pay attention to décor. You're wrong.
The way a space looks and feels is very important to men, because
the male brain is intensely visual-spatial. The right décor can even
convince a macho man to enter feminine territory—and pay to do it.

SportClips is a guy-oriented hair-cutting chain founded by a clever
man named Gordon Logan, who sensed men's discomfort with the
typical styling salon. Logan reasoned that guys would spend more
time and money in a place that was decorated according to their tastes.
SportClips looks and feels like a guy place—with flat-screen TVs, local
team jerseys, and locker room accessories throughout. By simply
changing the décor, SportClips has made the beauty parlor a masculine destination.

But many churches—particularly established ones—are decorated more like an old-fashioned ladies' beauty parlor. Quilted banners
and silk flower arrangements adorn church lobbies. More quilts, banners, and ribbons cover the sanctuary walls, complemented with fresh
flowers on the altar, a lace doily on the Communion table, and boxes
of Kleenex under every pew. And don't forget the framed Thomas
Kinkade prints, pastel carpets, and paisley furniture.

This femme décor sends a powerful subconscious message to
men: *you are out of place.* The moment men set foot in the vestibule,

they look around and get the same uneasy feeling they experience in a fabric store, a flower shop, or any other female-oriented locale.

You don't have to hang neon beer signs in church to get men comfortable. We'll discuss church décor options in chapter 16.

HAND-HOLDING AND HUGGING

Then there's hand-holding. Traditional churches often ask the faithful to reach across the aisles and hold hands with a neighbor. This attempt to model Christian unity can be awkward for men, especially those seated next to other men. Here's why. When a man holds hands, he takes the overgrip, while his wife assumes the undergrip. So when two men are asked to hold hands, there's an uncomfortable moment when they look each other in the eye and think, *Okay, who's going to be the girl?*

Certain churches are hug-rich environments. It's one thing for very close friends to embrace, but in some congregations it's customary for relative strangers to enfold. I once attended a church with an older gentleman who was a serial hugger. If he made eye contact, you were finished. He'd make a beeline for you, wrapping you in a bear hug before you could escape.

One man wrote columnist Judith Martin (Miss Manners) to say he'd stopped attending a church "where everybody seems to have developed a hugging addiction. Before the greeting period, the minister or lay leader stands on the platform and virtually orders everybody to get some hugs. People I hardly know run up to me and say, 'How about a hug?'"

Of course, there are many instances when man-to-man hugging is perfectly acceptable in church. I'll offer a few guidelines in chapter 22.

DRESS CODES

Some churches have an unwritten dress code: everyone must show up wearing Sunday best. This is another nod to femininity since women usually care more about their appearance and enjoy getting dolled up more than men do.

Fortunately, church dress codes are passing away. Informal dress is one of the hallmarks of the modern megachurch. More surprising still is a quiet revolution taking place in a few African-American churches, where being dressed for church has been as much a part of the religious experience as preaching and prayer. One black church in St. Louis changed its policy to "come as you are," and soon its male attendance tripled.[4]

PERSONAL EXPRESSION AND EMOTION

Smaller churches frequently offer their members an opportunity to express themselves during the worship service. The most common of these is called prayer-and-share. The pastor asks the congregation if anyone would like to share a joy or concern. The last time I attended a service with prayer-and-share, nine women and one man offered requests.

Prayer-and-share can be an irritant to men. Some congregations have a couple of magpies who stand up every week with some trivial thing to pray about: "Please pray for my Aunt Bessie's bunion." Others give too little information: "We need to keep praying for Gladys Hunt." (Men think, *Who the heck is Gladys Hunt, and why are we praying for her?*) Some requests are just boasting in disguise: "Please pray traveling mercies for my son. He's flying back to Harvard for the spring semester." You may also have a couple of wannabe preachers who take five minutes to share "what the Lord has laid on my heart." These are not prayer requests but sermonettes by people who want the spotlight. Such grandstanding rankles men.

In many Pentecostal churches individuals are encouraged to express themselves vigorously under the influence of the Holy Spirit. Shouting, running, pew-jumping, laughing, weeping, and swooning are common in smaller congregations. Even in the midst of a sermon, an individual may suddenly begin speaking in tongues in a loud voice. Everything halts while the one prophesying has his or her say. Then the pastor asks, "Do we have an interpretation?" After a few moments, another individual stands to deliver a "word from the Lord."

When Sam and Sally walk into a Spirit-filled church, emotions run high. Worshippers are expected to drop their guard and get jiggy with Jesus. Public display of emotion is much tougher for a guy because women are allowed to become outwardly emotional; men are not. Every young man learns this axiom: *big boys don't cry.* Strong men keep their emotions in check. Pentecostal men not only have to surrender to the Holy Ghost but must also break an ingrained social taboo.

I'm not condemning any of these things. I'm simply pointing out that personal expression during a worship service, no matter how well-intentioned, can be a barrier to men. At best, it takes the focus off of God and places it on the congregation. Women don't seem to mind this as much as men. Women tend to be more tolerant of personal expression, and are thrilled to learn what's going on in the lives of their friends. But men seem to prefer vertically focused worship—that is, up toward God. Personal expression makes the focus horizontal—across the aisle toward our neighbor.

At worst, personal expression gives visitors the impression that we're a little club of insiders (*Everyone knows Gladys Hunt; don't you?*). Personal expression can make a service run long, or cause men to feel their time is being wasted. (Men think, *I wish that blabbermouth would just sit down so we can move on.*) It can become a platform for the odd, disaffected, and imbalanced. Men notice something amiss when the interpretation is three times as long as the tongue. They see through the boasting, inconsistency, and hypocrisy, and then feel guilty for thinking ill of a fellow churchgoer.

In chapter 16, we'll see how a new breed of churches is creating vertical worship and horizontal fellowship at the same time.

Chapter 13

How Churches
Feminize over Time

THERE'S AN OLD WOMAN STANDING IN A PARKING LOT AT THE corner of Wilson Road and Edgecombe Boulevard. Her name is Norma. She's crying.

Norma is standing outside a medical supply store. It's housed in a squat, brick veneer structure with a peaked roof. She needs to buy a boot for her sprained ankle, but she simply can't bring herself to enter the building. It's not the pain in her leg that has her immobilized—it's the pain in her heart.

For more than three decades, this building was Norma's church. Two years ago, the church closed its doors.

The old Northside Church is now a medical supply store.

o o o

In the early 1950s, the area around Wilson Road was mostly farmland. A developer named George Edgecombe broke ground on Edgecombe Estates in March 1952.

Near the entrance to the neighborhood stood an old farmhouse. Rather than knock it down, Mr. Edgecombe donated the house and four acres of land to establish a church.

In September 1952, Northside Church began meeting in that

farmhouse. As Edgecombe Estates grew, so did the church. Members went door-to-door in the sparkling new neighborhood, inviting young families to church and leaving leaflets on the doors of those who weren't home. Soon about a dozen families from Edgecombe Estates were members of Northside. They invited their neighbors, and within a year, the old farmhouse was bursting with people every Sunday morning.

In 1955, Northside built a modest sanctuary. The church continued to use the farmhouse as Sunday school space until 1962, when it was demolished to make way for a new education/office wing. In 1968 the church built a larger sanctuary, turning the old one into a fellowship hall. Attendance continued to grow, and by 1975, Northside was welcoming more than 325 people on an average weekend and had a staff of four.

On September 18, 1977, Northside celebrated its twenty-fifth anniversary with the opening of a new gymnasium. That was also the peak year for attendance: nearly four hundred on an average weekend. Attendance remained stable for the next decade, but began slipping in the late 1980s. By 1991 just three hundred attended on an average Sunday. A decade later, Northside had fewer than one hundred attendees.

In 2008, the elders learned that Northside's facilities needed more than $200,000 in repairs and safety upgrades. With fewer than sixty regular attendees, Northside had no choice but to sell its property. The remaining members scattered to various churches in the area—including Norma, who is standing in front of the building, weeping.

o   o   o

Young churches start out with such vitality and promise. But over the years, they plateau and enter a slow decline. This year, thousands of US congregations will close their doors.

Most observers believe that old age is the main culprit. Churchgoers refuse to change with the times. Worship becomes old-fashioned, driving young people away. The congregation becomes self-focused and stops inviting new people. New racial and socioeconomic groups move into the area, but the church remains homogenous. Conflict splits churches, and they never recover.

But these are merely symptoms. I believe the root cause of these dysfunctions is the loss of masculine spirit. That loss, more than anything else, destroys a church from the inside out. It creates a vicious circle in which men depart, the church weakens, and more men depart. Once a church's adult attendance is 70 percent female, you can write its obituary.

o o o

Picture a major-league baseball player staring at a fastball sizzling toward the plate. He swings—*crack!* The ball leaves the end of the bat at more than 100 miles per hour. As the baseball soars, its speed diminishes and its arc levels out. For a brief moment it seems to hang in the air, its momentum mostly spent. Then the ball begins a slow descent, which gradually picks up speed as it falls into the waiting glove of the center fielder, just inside the warning track. One out.

The life span of a typical church resembles the arc of a long fly ball.

A healthy new church starts with a crack of energy. In the early years the congregation hurtles upward at 100 miles an hour. But over time the momentum slows. Somewhere in its third or fourth decade, the church plateaus—neither rising nor falling. Then, almost imperceptibly, the decline begins—slowly at first, but gaining speed after a few years. By now the descent is irreversible. Eventually the church crashes to earth. One out.

Of course, not every church follows this arc. Even mature churches can experience rebirth and growth. But the rise-plateau-decline arc is disturbingly common. Hardly anyone is talking about revitalizing old churches these days, because it so rarely succeeds. Instead, we're seeing an explosion of church planting in the US because young clergymen would rather ride the arc up—not down.

As pastor and church planter Mark Driscoll says, "It's a lot more fun making babies than it is resurrecting dead people."[1]

o o o

Back to the baseball metaphor. Ask a man, "Would you prefer to play offense or defense?" Most guys say, "Offense." Men would rather swing a bat than stand in the outfield.

Young churches have no choice but to play offense. Their survival depends on bringing new people in. A new church must adopt the values on the left side of this chart, or it will be dead in a year:

Young church (offense)	Established church (defense)
Grow or die	Growth is disruptive
External focus	Internal focus
Goal oriented	Gathering is the goal
Must bring in new people	Must keep existing people happy
Innovative	Predictable
High demand	Low demand
Lay empowered	Clergy driven
Strategic planning and building	Maintenance
Exists to achieve something	Exists as a network of relationships
Orthodox	Heterodox

Start-up congregations need men's gifts. Risks must be taken. Plans must be made. Buildings must be built. Men love this stuff. They have a lot to offer a young church. The grow-or-die culture of a young church buoys a man's spirit.

But once a church reaches a certain size, it stabilizes. The building gets finished, cash flow firms up, and a core membership is in place. At this point, the greatest need is not growth but maintenance.

The priority is no longer bringing in new members; it's keeping existing members volunteering and giving.

Slowly the offense leaves the field and the defense takes over. The switchover can take years. It happens one safe decision at a time, one predictable sermon at a time, one compromised belief at a time.

Eventually the church is no longer fishing for men. Instead, it's creating a comfortable aquarium for the saints. Members no longer go to church anticipating a life-altering encounter with God. Instead, they come to see friends and to participate in a comforting ritual that's changed little since childhood.

Although the pastor may want to play offense, his members force him to play defense. He spends a lot of time mediating disputes, smoothing ruffled feathers, and making people feel loved and affirmed. Hospital visitation, chairing meetings, and planning gatherings gobble up the rest of his time. Sure, he'd love to bring in more people, but the crisis of the moment is finding volunteers for Sunday school. Plus the Vickers family is mad about something he said in his sermon, and Sister Alice is upset because someone removed the doilies her late mother crocheted for the Communion table. The pastor is working sixty hours a week, and fifty-nine of those hours are focused inward, on his flock, who clamor endlessly for his attention.

The church stalls at the top of its arc—and the men notice first. They see little upward momentum. Theology and rules go squishy, as everyone must be kept happy. Because the people lack vision, trivial matters take on great importance. The inevitable squabbling, backbiting, and hypocrisy finally send men for the showers. Some leave the stadium.

Once the men check out (physically or emotionally), young men follow their example. Young women notice the lack of vitality in the church (and the lack of young men) and are next to leave.

That leaves faithful women age fifty and up. They stay with the team because the church is their relational network. They're invested in each other's lives, growing old together, and that wonderful fellowship is their manna. But after a few years even they notice the decline. Finally they begin whispering, "Where did all the young people go?"

Simple. Here's how it happened:

- Church shifts from offense to defense.
- Men get bored and disengage.
- Young men leave the church.
- Young women leave the church.
- Young couples visit; see few people their age.
- Nursery closes due to lack of children.
- Pews are filled with gray hair.

FROM KINGDOM TO FAMILY

Here's another way of seeing it: as churches become established, parishioners begin to shift from a *kingdom of God* mentality to a *family of God* mentality. They stop thinking of the church in terms of its mission and begin seeing it as an association of people who love each other. Kingdoms are about *doing*; families are about *being*.

The shift from kingdom to family thinking is not a conscious one. Parishioners still talk in kingdom language. The pastor still preaches about "winning the world for Jesus." But the church's actions reflect its true, family-of-God mentality. To illustrate, let's go back to Northside Church.

By 1983 attendance had been flat for five years. So the elders decided to switch to a new kind of outreach program that had done wonders for a sister church in a nearby city. But there was a problem: Northside already had an outreach program—that hadn't won a convert in years. This pitiful program was led by two dear saints who'd been in the church for decades: Brother Frank and Sister Dottie.

When these two heard that *their* ministry was on the chopping block, they became upset. They called their friends and accused the elders of being "dictatorial," "un-Christlike," and "power hungry." Before he knew what hit him, the pastor was inundated with complaints from angry members. The pastor went back to the elders, begging them to withdraw their proposal. They reluctantly agreed. Frank and Dottie's ineffective outreach program continued to meet and expend church funds. Church attendance continued to decline. Final score: Harmony 1, Effectiveness 0.

The elders were thinking with a kingdom-of-God mentality—how do we expand Jesus' reign on earth? But the people of Northside were thinking with a family-of-God mentality—how do we keep the family together, happy and harmonious? Sure, we want to bring in new people—but if that means hurting the feelings of our existing family members, then no thanks. In the end, the family of God triumphed over the kingdom of God (as it almost always does in well-established churches).

Here's a true story. I once served on the governing board of a church in Alaska. We had a prickly member who was always mad about something. Let's call her Sherry. Almost every month Sherry wrote an angry letter to the elders about this or that. We spent many hours discussing and addressing her grievances, often capitulating to her demands in a vain attempt to make her happy.

One day Sherry wrote the elders a scathing letter announcing she and her family were leaving to seek a new congregation. I remember looking around the table at the pained expressions of the elders as her letter was read. We spent about fifteen minutes wondering what we could have done differently. One elder agreed to write Sherry a letter of apology, asking her to reconsider her decision.

Then it was break time. I headed to the kitchen for a drink. Another elder came in right behind me. He broke into a broad smile, did a little dance, and offered me a high five. Then he said, "God bless Sherry—and God bless her new church!"

You may think it's cruel to celebrate the departure of a cranky church member, but I don't see it that way. Sherry was not renouncing her faith; she was simply moving on to another church. In a kingdom, this is standard procedure. The king moves his troops around as he sees fit. Soldiers are assigned to different platoons as the need arises. Personnel come and go. We say good-bye, we mourn, and we move on.

But in a family, we stay together through thick and thin. Family members don't come and go. The greatest tragedy is the loss of a member. It's like a death in the family.

Once a church adopts a family-of-God mentality, one ill-tempered member can literally hold the congregation hostage. By issuing a threat—to leave, to stop giving, or to stir up opposition—she can bend the entire church to her will. If the elders don't give in to her demands, she can gather a faction and threaten to start a family feud.

I've seen churchgoers issue threats over the most trivial things—a banner in the sanctuary, a ten-minute change in the start of a worship service, or the choice of VBS curriculum. Sad to say, the leaders often give in to the blackmailer.

This is why it's so hard to reinvigorate an ingrown church. The family mind-set is firmly entrenched. Everyone realizes change is badly needed—but change always upsets a family member. A threat is issued, and the leaders cave. Why? Because we can't face the possibility of a death in the family.

A healthy, kingdom-minded church does not negotiate with terrorists. When they threaten, strong leaders call their bluff. Leaders say, "We're sorry you're angry. We pray that God uses you mightily in your next church. Good-bye and God bless you." Healthy leaders see the departure of a member not as a death in the family, but as the king moving a soldier to another platoon.

o o o

The Kenai River in Alaska is home to some of the largest king salmon in the world. If you want to catch one of these monsters, you need a trolling motor—a small, low-energy propulsion device that provides just enough thrust to keep your boat in place as the current tries to push it downstream. Trolling motors are quiet and do not disturb the fish.

At this very moment your church is feminizing. It's being pushed by a natural, unstoppable current that propels congregations toward a family-of-God mentality. The same current pushes against every Christian institution, including universities, seminaries, and denominations. They are born orthodox, high demand, and externally focused. They die lenient, low demand, and focused on internal turf wars.

If you want to avoid being swept downstream, you need to troll. That is, you need constant vigilance to maintain a kingdom mindset. The final part of this book details the many ways a local church can launch a quiet, low-energy campaign to troll for men—without disturbing the fish in the aquarium.

Chapter 14

HOW CHURCHES DRIVE BOYS AWAY FROM THE FAITH

IT'S NO SECRET THAT WORSHIP SERVICES DO A POOR JOB TRANS-mitting faith to children in general—and to boys in particular. How has the church responded? With a flashing midway of specialized programs for the young: Sunday school, vacation Bible school, AWANA, CCD, confirmation classes, RAs and GAs, and youth group. Step right up, kids, and meet the *amazing* Jesus!

Despite this blizzard of programs aimed at youth, at least seven out of ten boys who are raised in this system leave the church during their teens and twenties.[1] Some alarmists believe we are witnessing a historic rejection of Christianity by the young.

Why is this happening? Certainly, worldly influences share some of the blame. Young men are bombarded with distractions and temptations their grandfathers could not imagine. Many of today's boys grow up fatherless or with irreligious dads. Then there's that perception that church is not for men—passed down to boys from role models, from the media, and from their peers.

Just as the adult church system caters to women, the Sunday school system has favored girls for decades. I'd like you to meet Connor, a twelve-year-old boy who has grown up in a traditional Sunday school program. Connor has just informed his mother that he hates Sunday school and never wants to go again. Why does Connor hate Sunday school? Even Connor doesn't know. After all, twelve-year-old boys are not practiced at the art of self-analysis.

Speaking as a former twelve-year-old boy, let me offer a theory: Connor is frustrated because, no matter how hard he tries, he cannot win in a traditional Sunday school class. And boys must have a chance to win—or they become discouraged and quit.

"Win" in Sunday school? You didn't realize it was a competition, did you?

With guys, everything is a competition. And here's the kicker: generally, men will only compete at things they're somewhat good at. If they have no chance of winning, they simply don't play.

One time I tried golf. You've heard of Tiger Woods? Well, I spent most of my time *in the woods*, looking for my ball. I have no knack for the game, so after a few rounds I gave it up. I knew I'd never be any good at it.

That's how Connor feels. After twelve years of nursery, preschool, and Sunday school, he knows he'll never really be good at church. To learn why Connor feels this way, let's rewind about six years.

o   o   o

Connor is a first grader. He's having trouble sitting still while his Sunday school teacher, Mrs. Lennon, tries to teach the class about Balaam and the talking donkey. Connor is bored and starts making donkey noises. The other kids think Connor is funny. Mrs. Lennon does not. She finally remands the disruptive boy to Mrs. Karl, the Sunday school superintendent. Connor spends the rest of the hour alone, playing with an ancient flannelgraph in the storage closet. (Connor sets Jesus to dive-bombing the disciples as they walk along the Sea of Galilee.)

On to second grade. Connor is supposed to be coloring a picture of Daniel in the lions' den. But instead, he's folded his paper into an airplane, which makes a perfect crash landing in Loretta Jenkins's ponytail. Connor and his friends are amused. Their teacher, Miss Ramirez, is not.

In third grade, Mrs. Carroll passes out well-worn King James Bibles to every student and then assigns each a passage to look up. Connor has the misfortune of drawing Daniel 1:1–7. As each student reads his or her verse, a pattern emerges: the girls are better than the boys at reading aloud. When Connor's turn finally comes, he's sweating with fear.

"In . . . the . . . third . . . year . . . of . . . the . . . reign . . . of . . . Jeh—Jeh-o—"

"Jehoiakim," says Mrs. Carroll.

"Jehoyakeem king . . . of . . . Ju-dah . . . came . . . Neb—Nebu—"

"Nebuchadnezzar."

"Nebu-kanezzer . . . king . . . of . . . Baby-lawn—"

The other kids titter. Mrs. Carroll shoots them a withering stare. "That's *Babylon.* Please continue, Connor."

In fourth grade, Connor's teacher, Mrs. Wilson, passes out those same Bibles. She teaches the youngsters a new game: sword drills. Mrs. Wilson barks out a Bible reference, such as, "First John 4:7–8. Go!" Bibles flip open; pages and fingers fly. The first student to find the passage jumps up and reads it to the rest of the class. You can probably guess which gender usually jumps first.

Connor usually likes competition, but he's not very good at this game. It combines two of his weaknesses: reading aloud and fine motor skills. Girls often read better than boys and do so at an earlier age. And throughout their lives, women have greater finger dexterity than men. Connor's clumsy boy fingers aren't very good at flipping through fine onionskin pages. One time he thought he found a verse, but he read from John's gospel instead of John's first epistle. Disqualified.

In fifth grade, Connor is assigned the role of a wise man in the Sunday school Christmas pageant. He has to wear a fake beard and sing a solo. Connor is chosen because he's one of the few boys who still attend Sunday school regularly. Connor feels like a fool wearing a towel over his head and dyed cotton balls on his face. Somehow he manages to get through his part, delivering his lines with the enthusiasm of a convict headed for the gallows.

So by sixth grade, Connor is tired of Sunday school. He's tired of being outshone by the girls. He's tired of being embarrassed. Sunday school makes him feel dumb. Connor would rather do the things he's good at, like running around on a soccer field, kicking a ball.

That's where more and more Connors can be found on Sunday morning. Sports leagues are taking over the time slot traditionally occupied by church. This is fine with boys. They know how to win on the athletic field. But in Sunday school, it's very hard for boys to win. The rules favor children who can sit quietly, read aloud, memorize verses, and look up passages in books. A star pupil is also compliant, empathetic, and sensitive. A long attention span and the ability to receive verbal input from a female teacher also help.

How many ten-year-old boys do you know who fit this description?

Oddly enough, there is a boy like this in Connor's Sunday school class. Brian is a quiet, obedient kid. He's a bit of a nerd. Brian is very studious and loves to read. He grew up in a devout home, so he knows his Bible. Brian is not particularly athletic; he's more the artistic type. He's kindhearted and empathetic. Brian is very close to his mom.

Fast-forward thirteen years. Brian graduates from seminary and becomes a pastor.

o o o

Boys, like men, are visual creatures. They believe what they see. Unfortunately, the Jesus they see in church and Sunday school is warping their impression of God.

Traditional holy pictures portrayed Jesus as thin, pale, and soft, with long, flowing tresses caressing an androgynous face. This Jesus bears little resemblance to the rugged Judean carpenter who possessed the strength to drive out the money changers with a whip. Catholic boys meet Jesus at his weakest moment: half-dead, stripped, head down, and nailed to a cross. (Meanwhile the female icon, the Blessed Virgin, always looks healthy, calm, and serene. Hm.)

But the old holy pictures did get one thing right: they showed Jesus as a man of action—working in the company of men. Sure, they wore robes and had long, flowing hair, but at least they had beards.

In the 1980s, a Sunday school curriculum publisher decided to do some market research. He discovered that most of his product was purchased by married, middle-aged women. So he asked these ladies what they disliked about traditional curriculum. They spoke with one voice: "The pictures!" They thought Christ seemed frightening and unkind. Instead, they preferred to see pictures of a friendly Jesus doing fun things—preferably smiling, with children on his lap.

The publisher immediately called in his artists and ordered them to give Jesus a makeover. Out went the somber Nazarene in the company of men—replaced by a happy Jesus loving children.

The new Jesus was an instant hit. Women rushed to purchase this updated curriculum. Soon every Sunday school publisher had remade Jesus into a smiling Jewish camp counselor.

But there was a problem with the new Jesus. He took wimpishness to a new level—particularly when you compared him to the tough guys boys idolize. The male action heroes of popular entertainment are hypermasculine, scowling, and filthy, with sweat shining off their bulging muscles. Meanwhile, the new Jesus looked as if he'd just come from a spa treatment.

Once again, modern marketing created a Jesus who does not exist. The true Christ of Scripture is more akin to a gritty superhero. As a homeless man, he was no stranger to sweat and grime. As a tradesman, he must have been well muscled. Like a video game hero, Jesus was a fighter who left a trail of mayhem in his wake. He vanquished demons, destroyed stuff, and made people so mad they tried to kill him.[2] Camp counselors don't get nailed to crosses.

Not only was the new Jesus sissy, but most of the new illustrations placed him in the presence of children. And what's wrong with that? Nothing—as long as you also show Jesus among men. But over the past twenty years, Jesus-and-the-children imagery has come to dominate Sunday school curriculum. In the lower grades, it's practically the only picture of Christ children see.

All these pictures of the Messiah chillin' with children have created an unbreakable subconscious link between Christ and childhood in the minds of boys. As young men mature and think of Jesus, their mind's eye recalls those images of him with little ones. The time bomb is planted.

When a boy reaches puberty, desperate to become a man, the bomb explodes. A voice in his head says, *Christ is for children. I'm no longer a child. Therefore, I must rid myself of Christ.* We have an epidemic of young men leaving the faith not because they disbelieve, but because they perceive Christ to be a pansy and church to be a symbol of childhood.

Clever marketing has done its damage—by catering to the women who buy curriculum, publishers have unwittingly sabotaged the faith of young men.

Girls are largely unaffected because they never reject their childhoods the way boys do. It's not uncommon for a seventeen-year-old girl to display stuffed animals, dolls, and baby pictures in her room. Seventeen-year-old boys never do this. Every young man comes to the day when he puts away childish things.[3] And thanks to the way we portray Jesus in Sunday school, Christ has become a childish thing.

o o o

The real tragedy is not just that we're losing boys—we are losing the most competitive, aggressive boys. High-testosterone boys destined to be leaders and innovators are checking out of church at a young age. Worldly temptations play a role, to be sure. But many disengage simply because of the way we raise them in the faith. They cannot compete in Sunday school, so they drop out. We teach them Christ is for children, so they drop out.

Thank heaven for high school youth group. That's been the salvation of generations of young men. I became a Christian at the age of fifteen, thanks to a youth group.

When I was an adolescent, youth group was fun. It was based on the three Gs: *games, goofiness,* and *God.* We sang simple songs. We played nutty games. The teaching time was brief but meaningful to teens. I loved it. And it attracted a lot of guys. Church services were sometimes boring, but youth group was always a kick.

In the 1970s and '80s, youth group music was simple and light-hearted. All you needed was a guitar and three or four songs. The first two songs were usually goofy ("Give me wax on my board, keep me surfin' for the Lord"). The second two were more serious ("I wish we'd all been ready"). The singing was usually done in about ten minutes. Then it was time for "the talk." Youth leaders of the 1970s understood guys. My youth leader used to tell us, "Christianity, properly practiced, will result in your death."

Praise and worship arrived in youth group during the early 1990s. The goofy songs disappeared. Singing time expanded to thirty minutes or more. Songs flowed from one to another. Sometimes the guitarist would pause, waiting for someone to start singing a cappella, "as they felt led." The whole feeling changed from a fun group activity to an intimate personal time with God. Youth leader "talks" came to focus on sexual purity and relationships.

In the 2000s, the praise band came to youth groups. Today, even small churches are putting together youth rock bands. Big churches are remodeling their youth spaces to offer professional quality stages, lighting, and sound equipment.

The youth meeting is quickly evolving into a music-centric experience. Youth stand in a darkened room and sing love songs to Jesus, led by a praise band of their peers. Singing can occupy up to half of the meeting. This has been great for the musicians—they get lots of stage time. But for the nonmusical, lengthy singing can be a drag.

Girls thrive in this emotional hothouse, but most boys melt and evaporate. Before you know it, you've got nineteen girls and five guys at youth group. And there's not a jock among the guys.

By their senior year, girls are 14 percent more likely to have participated in a youth group. And they are 21 percent more likely to have stayed involved in youth group all four years of high school.[4] Congratulations. The stage is set for the female-dominated church of the future.

o o o

Youth group was once a thing apart. But it's quickly evolving into another church service—built upon a familiar format: singing and a sermon. I call it *church lite*. Youth ministry has become a development league for future pastors and music ministers. Never mind that church lite is a disaster for most boys—and up to 80 percent of kids who are raised in youth group abandon the church by age twenty-nine.[5] We do church lite because preachers-and-worship-leaders-in-training need stage time before they're called up to the big leagues.

Why is a church lite youth group so injurious to boys? It's a very sedentary experience. It's a lot of singing, sitting, and listening. It's designed to stimulate the mind and emotions, leaving the body out of the equation.

What's wrong with this? Boys are kinetic creatures. Young men need to move. During their teens, boys' bodies are awash in testosterone. It makes them aggressive, risk taking, and fidgety. Healthy kinetic activity is one of the keys to unlocking a young man's heart.

Paul Hill, David Anderson, and Roland Martinson are authors of an extensive study of the spiritual lives of young men. They found that young men's "quest for identity and spirituality is kinesthetic—experienced through their bodies as much as their minds. With only a few exceptions, this was true regardless of race, class or context for the young men in our study."[6]

One need only to watch Muslims at prayer to understand the power that body movement exerts in the spiritual lives of men. Yet 90 percent of Christian worship involves standing still or sitting still, either singing songs or listening to a teacher. So unless a young man is studious, sensitive, or musical, he'll probably find a church lite youth group boring—regardless of what's being taught—because his body is not moving enough.

The whole youth group package is boy-repellent. Young men feel oddly out of place but don't know why. Standing in a darkened room for twenty-five minutes, singing love songs to a man, feels pointless at best. Endless "talks" about relationships and purity do nothing to fire their imaginations. Some secretly wonder, *I'm supposed to like this, but I'm just not into it. Is there something wrong with me?*

o o o

Nonetheless, there are signs of hope. Some youth ministry programs are working. Children's Sunday school is changing—for the better. We will discuss these successful efforts in chapter 21.

PART 3

CALLING THE CHURCH BACK TO MEN

A ROCK CLIMBER CAN SCALE A SHEER CLIFF FACE IF HE HAS ENOUGH handholds and footholds. The holds don't have to be large—just frequent enough to allow him to get a little closer to the summit.

So it is in church: a couple of masculine footholds can help a man feel at home in a house of worship. But as we've seen, churches have been removing the masculine footholds for generations.

So what's a foothold? Sometimes it's as simple as this: A joyful woman recently told me that her husband had returned to the church after more than a decade as a lost sheep. Naturally, I asked her why he came back to the fold. "Well, the Sunday he decided to visit, our pastor used a golf club as an illustration," she said. "My husband is an avid golfer, and he said he could really relate to that sermon. He's been coming ever since."

We don't have to make the church something it's not. There's no need for knife-throwing during Communion or hand-to-hand combat during the offertory. Men just need to know they're valued.

Christian laymen have felt ignored or invisible in church for a long time. They want footholds. They want to climb.

How do I know? Churches that reestablish the masculine footholds are seeing men return. These guys are bringing growth, innovation, and dynamism with them.

o o o

June 6, 1944, was D-day—the greatest military assault in modern history. The allies were determined to retake a continent that had fallen to Nazi tyranny.

Exactly one hundred years prior to D-day—June 6, 1844—the battle to restore men to the church began in London. The next eleven chapters are the story of that battle—a battle that continues to this day.

Chapter 15

THE BATTLE TO
REENGAGE MEN

AT THE DAWN OF THE INDUSTRIAL REVOLUTION, LARGE NUMBERS
of men began disappearing from local congregations. Churches
became bastions of female presence and power. Feminized, bookish
men came to dominate the clergy. One observer described Victorian
preachers as "pallid, puny, sedentary, and lifeless."

Something had to be done.

The battle to reengage men began June 6, 1844. A twenty-two-year-
old farmer-turned-department-store-worker named George Williams
gathered eleven friends and organized the first Young Men's Christian
Association, a refuge of Bible study and prayer for young men seeking
escape from the dangers of tenement housing and life on the streets of
London.[1]

Williams was not trying to spark a masculine counter-
revolution in the church. He simply saw men who needed Christ.
But his YMCA grew rapidly, spread to the United States, and became
the first of dozens of initiatives designed to relink manliness and
godliness. Together these efforts came to be known as the Muscular
Christianity movement.

Muscular Christianity was a direct assault on Puritan notions
of piety. During the Colonial era (1600s and 1700s), Christians had
developed a mistrust of anything physical. Many clergymen felt that

127

recreation, sporting, and competition distracted from spiritual pursuits such as Bible reading and prayer. Physical conditioning was frowned upon because of the corruptibility and impermanence of the flesh. Fun and pleasure were out; serious theological discourse was in.

So imagine the furor when the Young Men's Christian Association built its first gymnasium in the name of Christ, in 1869. Sixteen years later, the YMCA opened America's first rural summer camp at Orange Lake, New York. In 1881, a Boston YMCA staffer coined the term *bodybuilding*. YMCA staff and volunteers invented the games of basketball, volleyball, and racquetball.

The YMCA also reached out to soldiers by serving as chaplains and medical corpsmen during the Civil War. In the late 1800s the Y began offering vocational courses to men, and at one time operated twenty colleges in cities around the country. In an era of strict racial segregation, YMCAs reached out to men of all colors and cultural backgrounds. YMCAs became known for offering wholesome over-night lodging at affordable prices—and during the 1920s and '30s offered more overnight accommodations than any other hotel chain in America.

Founder George Williams once said, "If a young man says he has lost God, first buy him dinner." The YMCA's strategy was to lure young men back to the faith by linking spiritual health to physical well-being. Gymnasiums, camps, and comfortable beds were merely the bait.

Local churches saw the success of the YMCA and began copying it. Today, we think nothing of a church having a gym, but it was considered radical when the first church gymnasiums started appearing in the late 1800s. Denominations began acquiring the rural parcels that are still church recreational camps today. Christian ministers coined a new word to describe the ideal man: *masculine*.

In the United States, the Businessman's Awakenings of 1857–58 were believed to be the first evangelistic outreach aimed specifically at males. The great evangelist D. L. Moody cut his teeth at the Chicago Awakening and spent the rest of his career targeting men with his preaching. Athletes-turned-evangelists such as Billy

Sunday crisscrossed the country, winning tens of thousands of male converts. Sunday drew criticism from genteel ministers for "doffing his coat, breaking furniture and employing sports metaphors" as he preached. "But others welcomed Sunday's claim that one could be both a Christian and a 'real man.'"[2]

In 1865, William Booth launched an entire church denomination built upon a masculine metaphor. Booth called his church The Salvation Army. Although the Army did not set out to reach men specifically, its structure and discipline has enthralled generations of them. And today, with only six hundred thousand members, the Salvation Army sponsors missions in one hundred nations and helps more needy people than every other denomination combined.

At the turn of the twentieth century, churchmen were alarmed to discover up to 80 percent of the boys raised in Sunday school abandoned it during their teens.[3] So a host of ministries sprang up to reach these lads, including Boys' Brigade, the Knights of King Arthur, and of course, the Boy Scouts. These groups were formed to keep God uppermost in the minds of young men who saw themselves as too cool for Sunday school.

Despite decades of outreach to men, by 1910, US church attendance was still running two-thirds female. Midweek participation figures were even more lopsided.[4] Concern over Christianity's man-gap went all the way to the White House, where President Theodore Roosevelt became a supporter of the Men and Religion Forward Movement, a short-lived series of Christian men's rallies held in cities around the United States in the years before World War I.

THE MANLY MAINLINE?

Believe it or not, the liberal mainline churches were the greatest exponents of Muscular Christianity. These churches (Episcopal, Methodist, Lutheran, Presbyterian, and United Church of Christ) were the first to build gyms and sponsor sports leagues and wilderness camps. They also focused attention on something they called the Social Gospel: performing good works outside the walls of the church.

What did Muscular Christianity achieve? In its first hundred years (1844–1944) it did not bring gender balance to the church—but it kept the score close. The movement spawned a number of Christian organizations that engaged men on the fringe. But perhaps its greatest legacy was the spectacular success of the mainline churches after World War II.

When the builder generation returned from the war, men flooded back into church. And men chose the mainline. Many Catholics defected to the mainline (my own father among them). Irreligious men affiliated with the mainline. During the 1950s, American men found it quite acceptable to be an Episcopalian, a Presbyterian, a Methodist, or a Lutheran.

Why did men choose the mainline? After a century of building gyms, sponsoring men's outreach, and promoting the Social Gospel, the mainline had established trust and brand loyalty among men. And as men poured in, mainline churches exploded in size and influence. Church growth expert Lyle Schaller's 1952 survey found adult attendance in America's mainline was 53 percent female, 47 percent male, mirroring the US population.[5] During the 1960s, mainline church members were actually younger than the population as a whole.[6]

But then, inexplicably, the mainline began turning its back on all things masculine. By the mid-1960s, mainline churches began focusing inward, losing their evangelistic fervor. Ministry to women and children grew, but men's ministry stagnated. Women became elders and eventually pastors. Predictably, men began vacating church boards and denominational power structures. Mainline seminaries abandoned traditional orthodoxy and became dispensaries of anti-war, left-wing ideology. By the 1980s, mainline denominations were gender-neutralizing their liturgies, songs, and scriptures.

Today, the mainline is fractured with dissention—bleeding members and losing influence. No one seems able to make a decision. Mainliners fight the same battles year after year, papering over differences in the name of "unity and peace." And just as an Episcopal rector wrote in 1856, "The church is composed chiefly of females and aged men."[7]

So the man-heavy church of the 1950s and '60s was an anomaly. Men have been less interested in the Christian faith for centuries. Men have had the pulpit; women have had the pews.

o o o

When tens of thousands of Christian men began gathering in stadiums during the 1990s, many believers thought they were witnessing something new. Some called Promise Keepers "a fresh move of God among men."

Not really. PK was simply another salvo in a battle that's been raging since 1844. Promise Keepers is not the first high-profile effort to bring men back to church—and it certainly won't be the last. And just like its predecessors, it was questioned by the church establishment, suspected by clergymen, and embraced by the remnant of men who desperately sought reinforcements in their dwindling ranks.

I'll wrap up this chapter with a quote from a man who used to torture me once a month. His name was Dr. L. S. McGuffey—my orthodontist. McGuffey hung a plaque in his examination room that read, "Ignore your teeth . . . and they'll go away."

So it is with men. When churches ignore their men, they soon find themselves without many. Donations, volunteerism, evangelism, and attendance all suffer. But give men a little attention, and they respond. The church grows. In the next chapter I'll show you a new species of church that has figured this out—and is flourishing as a result.

Chapter 16

WHY MEGACHURCHES
ARE MEGA

IN CASE YOU HADN'T NOTICED, BIG CHURCHES ARE GETTING BIG-
ger. They're expanding their "campuses" and going "multisite." The
percentage of Americans who attend a megachurch has never been
higher. Meanwhile, the vast majority of traditional churches are not
growing. They watch in resignation as their young people drop
out—or defect to the megas.

Experts define a megachurch as one that draws more than two
thousand attendees on a typical weekend. In 1970, there were fewer
than twenty megachurches in the United States. Forty years later that
number had risen to about fourteen hundred megachurches—and it
continues to grow. The largest 20 percent of US churches have about
65 percent of the money, resources, and people.[1]

Megachurch fans say they're relevant. They're up-to-date. They
care for their communities. Megachurch critics say they're shallow.
They water down the gospel. They're just a show.

I'm not going to wade into this debate. Love them or hate them,
megachurches do get at least one thing right: they attract men. As
we saw in chapter 2, the larger the congregation, the less likely it is
to have a man shortage.[2]

But men are not just a by-product of church growth—they are
the reason behind it.

Men are Miracle-Gro for a church. Put men in a church and it will grow. The men don't even have to be that committed. We saw this a generation ago. Mainline churches in postwar America scooped up religiously adrift men—and grew like mad as a result. But during the 1970s, the mainline turned its back on men (and all things masculine). Almost immediately mainline churches began deflating like leaky balloons—losing members and influence.

Now the megachurches (and church plants) have taken a page from the 1950s mainline. They've become the new landing pad for disconnected men. As a result, they're growing like crazy. Fifty years ago, mainline pastors were the most influential voices for religion in America; today, megachurch pastors are.

The good news is any church can attract and retain men. You don't need a twelve-million-dollar campus, a thirty-by-forty video screen, or a pastor with a goatee. Any church, regardless of its size, staffing, and budget, can do it. But it's not enough to copy one or two things they're doing at the megachurch. You have to create a culture that welcomes men. Again, there's no need to alter the gospel, Jesus, doctrines, or core beliefs. Here's the story of how a famous megachurch founder created that culture.

o o o

In 1975 a twenty-three-year-old youth leader named Bill Hybels spent weeks going door-to-door in the Chicago suburbs, asking people why they didn't go to church. He heard the usual excuses. "It's boring and irrelevant." "It's a guilt trip." "They ask for money too much." "There are too many hypocrites."

When Hybels dug deeper, he found that many women were willing to go to church, but their husbands resisted. Furthermore, these men self-identified as Christians but were reluctant to practice their faith in public. Hybels had a revelation:

1. The key to reaching unchurched families was to reach husbands.

2. The key to reaching husbands was to create a church where men weren't embarrassed to worship.
3. Once Dad was in the door, the family would happily follow.

Hybels founded Willow Creek Community Church in suburban Chicago in 1975. Early on, Hybels created a mythical target parishioner named "Unchurched Harry." Hybels built the church's entire culture around Harry, making every decision to get Harry in the door and to make him feel at home once he was there.[3]

A few years later, a young, penniless Baptist preacher did virtually the same thing in Southern California. Rick Warren founded Saddleback Church after going door-to-door. He launched his church in a condo in 1980, and today Saddleback may be the most influential church on earth.

Warren built his congregation around the needs and expectations of a man named "Saddleback Sam." Sam is a busy professional in his early forties. He's college educated, married, and the father of two kids. He likes his job, his house, and his station in life. He prefers casual to formal. He's overextended in both time and money. He'd rather be in a large group than a small one. He's skeptical of organized religion. Warren realized that if guys like Sam came to Saddleback, the church would grow and prosper.[4]

Thousands of church planters have followed the lead of Willow Creek and Saddleback. Whether they realize it or not, popular church-planting models are designed to engage men. It's not that women don't matter—they do. But men are the crucial deciders when it comes to church involvement. Men are the first domino that must fall.

On its face, this strategy sounds radical (or sexist). But Christ did the same thing. He did not recruit a diverse group of men, women, and children. Instead, he focused like a laser on a homogenous group of twelve guys. Men like Simon Peter became the "rock" upon which he built his church. Diversity and increase came later.

So what's the megachurch formula for reaching men? It starts with the founding pastor.

MEGACHURCH FOUNDERS DRAW MEN

Men who establish large churches are, by definition, risk takers. It takes insane boldness to plant a church with no building, no paycheck, and no congregation. That boldness permeates the organization—and makes the church attractive to men.

Founding pastors are empire builders. I mean this in the kindest sense. While a few are in it for impure motives, the vast majority are in it for God. These talented men could be making big money in corporate America, but they've chosen to risk it all on Jesus' promise of heavenly reward. Their biggest thrill is seeing lives transformed and souls saved. They want the hundredfold increase Christ promised.

Megachurch founders are visionaries who care little about tradition—only about effectiveness. A good way to describe them is "restless innovators."

Big church pastors are gifted communicators who know how to hold an audience's attention. They have an innate ability to make Bible truth sound unreligious. Francis Chan took the shopworn phrase "God is love" and expressed it for a new generation: *Crazy Love*. Erwin McManus renamed the gospel *The Barbarian Way*.

Unfortunately, some megachurches are personality cults, built on the charisma of the founding pastor. When he steps down—*poof!*—the church disappears. That's one of the big raps on seeker-friendly churches—they're a mile wide and an inch deep.

MEGACHURCHES ARE FREE TO INNOVATE

Ever wonder why mainline churches are having such a hard time modernizing? High Church governance structures are designed to slow the pace of change. They were devised centuries ago, before the days of telecommunication, when isolated congregations could easily spin off into heresy. To ensure theological fidelity, denominations built in several levels of control. For example, every Presbyterian congregation is under four levels of authority: the session, the presbytery, the synod, and the general assembly.

Slow, deliberate decisions were a big advantage two centuries ago. But in today's lightning-paced society, bureaucratic structures are causing traditional churches to fall behind. They cannot quickly implement good ideas or kill bad ones because it's so hard to get a decision. Innovation comes slowly, and in half measures.

That enormous governance structure requires a lot of meetings that quite frankly accomplish little. When I served as an elder in a Presbyterian church, one of my greatest frustrations was the amount of time I spent in meetings—as opposed to helping people know and follow Christ.

Meanwhile, nondenominational churches zoom forward—trying new things, grasping opportunities, and changing methods to meet immediate needs. These churches are free to be creative because they are liberated from external control. (Southern Baptist churches are also congregationally autonomous, and their ability to innovate has helped them hold attendance steady even as the mainline has declined.)

Megachurches Are Obsessed with Quality

When men think of church, *excellence* and *quality* are often the last two words that come to mind. In fact, church has a reputation for mediocrity in the minds of many men. Guys are turned off by amateurish music, worn-out facilities, and unkempt grounds. Lee Strobel puts it this way: "I've been at churches where paint was peeling from the walls, sound systems were plagued by distortion, lighting was so dim I could barely see the face of the speaker, musicians read their lyrics instead of having them memorized, and the message sounded as if it were ad-libbed."[5]

If there's one word to describe the ethos of the modern megachurch, it's *quality*. Why is quality so important? Because church growth depends on people inviting their friends. Men will not invite their friends to a church service that's corny, hokey, or half-baked. John Lewis has dubbed this the "cringe factor"—defining it as "what happens when a Christian finally gets up enough nerve to invite his unbelieving friend to church, and the Christian quietly cringes through the service because of the off-key singing, out-of-tune piano, bad acoustics, malfunctioning microphones, and disjointed sermon."[6]

Small churches often take a karaoke approach to music, letting anyone perform, regardless of talent. A friend of mine once said, "I've sat through many kiddie violin solos and pitiful piano offertories. The mothers in the congregation think these are adorable, but we men do not." Even worse are adults who perform but lack talent. Family churches let tone-deaf Tanya "make a joyful noise," regardless of her ability to carry a tune. Men who visit the church don't know what a dear soul Tanya is. They just know the music is bad, and they don't come back.

Bob Russell, retired pastor of the eighteen-thousand-member Southeast Christian Church, asks, "Why have our people been so bold in inviting their friends and so effective in getting them to come? Because they are excited about what they've experienced and are confident that every week the grounds, the nursery, the greeting, the singing, and the preaching will be done with excellence."[7] Eliminate the cringe factor, and men will feel more comfortable inviting their friends.

MEGACHURCHES SPEAK MEN'S LANGUAGE

Men see their values emphasized in big churches. These congregations speak the language of risk, productivity, and growth. They become known in the community. Big churches measure effectiveness, celebrate achievement, and are constantly launching new projects and initiatives to capture men's hearts.

Big church pastors use masculine metaphors and language. They invite people to "join the team" and "get into the game." Megachurch pastors don't preach sermons; they deliver messages. Many of these messages are targeted right at men. Christ's Church of the Valley in Phoenix titled two popular sermon series "Warrior" and "Sex Drive."

IMAGE, BRANDING, AND DÉCOR

Megachurches are blasted for being image conscious. It sounds so unspiritual to talk about branding in the church. Honestly, can you imagine Jesus worrying about his brand?

But megachurches are simply acknowledging the truth: churches have been branding themselves since Martin Luther tacked his ninety-five theses on the Wittenburg door. The post-Reformation brands were Anabaptist, Puritan, Congregationalist, Quaker, and Calvinist. These gave way to a second wave of brands: Presbyterian, Episcopal, Methodist, Church of Christ, Nazarene, Assembly of God, Baptist, and many others.

Bill Hybels and Rick Warren realized unchurched people were turned off by the established church brands of the 1970s. These labels meant "boring, old-fashioned, guilt-inducing, and money-grubbing." They suggested separatism and competition. So the early megachurches branded around the word *community*: Willow Creek Community Church. Saddleback Community Church. Some have dropped the word *church* from their names altogether: Mosaic. Imago Dei. Lifepoint. Crossroads. The Vineyard.

Church plants understand the power of imagery. Their logos are often gritty, stark trademarks that would look right at home on a skateboard. They have image-driven websites that allow people to check them out from a distance. (Small churches—invest in a good website. It can make your church seem cooler than it really is.)

Megachurches refer constantly to their mission and purpose. They are not shy about celebrating "what God is accomplishing in our midst." And they talk about organized religion as if it were a disease.

All this branding is targeted at one person: the skittish man who's interested in God, but not church. It's designed to say, "Check us out. We understand you. We're up-to-date. We're not going to jam a Bible down your throat."

Big Man on "Campus"

Megachurches work hard on the front-door experience. They realize that the church must make a good impression from the moment a person drives into the parking lot. They keep their grounds meticulously groomed. Megachurches recruit enthusiastic men to serve as parking attendants, not because people need help parking their cars, but because they want visitors to see men serving and enjoying themselves. They post signs everywhere, so visiting men never have to ask for directions. There are greeters at every entrance to offer a welcoming handshake or a pat on the back.

Megachurch "campuses" don't look like churches. You're not likely to find statues, bell towers, or steeples. The campus often resembles a conference center, a coffee house, a rock concert hall, or a theater. There's often a large lobby with a high ceiling (so men don't feel trapped). Many paint their walls in man-friendly earth tones, complemented with natural wood or stone accents. Worship spaces are usually devoid of religious symbols, such as stained glass, crosses, and descending doves.

Everything is meticulously clean and cared for. There are no unclaimed Bibles sitting in stacks in the entryway. No stains in the carpet (despite the fact that coffee is welcome everywhere).

Large churches have a buzz of success about them that men find attractive. The moment you walk in you sense energy, forward movement, purpose, and drive. Because the megachurch does everything with professionalism, it tends to attract a higher percentage of successful, well-educated parishioners. These folks tend to earn more. The megachurch puts these folks through Crown Financial or Dave Ramsey anti-debt courses, which shores up their finances and allows them to become more responsible givers, which pays for the multimillion-dollar campus.

OUT WITH THE MAN-REPELLENT STUFF

It's not just what megachurches have added—it's what they've subtracted that brings in men.

Gone is the homespun décor so common in family churches. There's not a quilt, a felt banner, or a needlepoint on any wall. The Communion table has disappeared, along with the lace tablecloth and flower arrangements that adorned it. Megachurches tightly control what's posted on interior walls, whereas small churches allow handmade signs, photo collages, or school-type bulletin boards that suggest a kindergarten classroom.

Megachurches don't make their guests sing anything, say anything, or sign anything. Nor do they ask members to hug or hold hands. Some have even dispensed with the "turn and greet your neighbor" time. Small churches often ask visitors to stand and be welcomed, but megachurches never do this, allowing men to come and go anonymously. The dress code is "come as you are." *Informality* is the watchword.

A large church's greatest weakness—difficulty creating warmth and intimacy—is actually a plus for a lot of men. Most guys enjoy the anonymity of a large church. They can attend Sunday worship while avoiding the pressure to get involved that might hound them in a smaller church.

Vertical Focus

Small churches often try to create a hybrid worship/small group care experience on Sunday morning. They focus on God through prayer, worship, and the sermon. But they also care for individuals by taking prayer requests and announcements from the audience. They call new and departing members forward to be recognized. They sometimes stop and pray for folks with needs.

But in trying to accomplish two things (vertically focused worship and horizontally focused caring) the hybrid model is often less effective than it could be. Only a few individuals get cared for on Sunday morning. And the congregation's focus swings back and forth from God to people.

Megachurches have realized it's impossible to deliver both high-quality worship and small group care in a weekly service. So they've split these into two parts: a vertically focused worship service, and a horizontally focused midweek small group. Sunday worship is big, celebratory, and impersonal; Tuesday night group is small, relational, and intimate. In other words, Sunday worship is about the kingdom of God; Tuesday night group is about the family of God. This two-pronged strategy allows megachurches to provide everyone with a higher-quality worship experience, while giving every small group attendee the opportunity to be cared for and encouraged.

MEN ON STAGE

I did a little experiment last summer. I visited the five fastest-growing churches in our city. Every one of them showcased men in prominent roles. Men were conspicuous in every aspect of the worship service: leading worship, ushering, giving testimonies, and teaching. All five churches had male pastors. One church had an all-male praise band. One even had men in charge of the children's ministry.

Women weren't invisible in these churches, but men were given the high-profile spots in the worship service. Why? When a man sees enthusiastic men in leadership, he is likely to believe there is a place for him in church. Women also appreciate animated male leaders because they are such a rarity in modern society.

GUY-FRIENDLY ELEMENTS

Megachurch services are creative. Prayers are brief and conversational. There's often an element of humor. Guys dig this stuff.

Megachurches make sure the service moves along. No dead time between elements. The service starts and ends on time.

And what about those large projection screens? We laugh, but they're a boon to men's learning style. Once again, the male brain is visual-spatial, whereas the female brain is more verbal. Women are stimulated by words; men are stimulated by images. Megachurches are restoring visual elements to worship centuries after Protestant reformers, in a wave of anti-Catholic zeal, stripped the sanctuary bare.

Of course, not everything is completely man-friendly in the megachurch. Although the quality of the music is always superb, as we saw in chapter 9, contemporary worship can be challenging to men. Twenty-minute worship sets of unfamiliar or unsingable music can test the patience of any man. There are too many sermons about relationships, and not enough about mission. And the big rap on megachurches is partly true: their audiences are full of spectators instead of participators.

But by and large, the megachurches are doing right by men. And the presence of men is foundational to their explosive growth.

o o o

All right, you small-church members. The purpose of this chapter is not to say, "Megachurches are doing everything right, and you're doing everything wrong." It's simply my attempt to pull back the curtain and show you the hidden secret to their meteoric growth—men.

And here's the good news: you don't have to be a megachurch to get guys. Churches of all sizes can attract men and experience the growth and health they bring.

As my friend Kenny Luck, men's minister at Saddleback Church, likes to say, "There is no move of God without men of God." If you want the Lord to move in your church, go for the guys.

Chapter 17

PASTORS AND MEN

WHEN I WAS IN COLLEGE, I WONDERED IF GOD MIGHT BE CALLING me to the ministry. But when I discovered how demanding a pastor's life really is, I decided God must have dialed a wrong number.

Pastors, I admire you. You have a complex, largely thankless job. I can't think of any profession that pulls a person in more directions than the pastorate. Leading a church is like trying to play cards in a hurricane, and seminary prepared you to preach, not lead. You may be frustrated by the lack of male participation in your congregation, or you may be uncertain how to get men involved.

Here's a truth about men that will either thrill you or terrify you. Men don't follow religions. Men don't follow philosophies. Men don't follow ideas.

Men follow men.

Every man is, at his core, a hero worshipper. And you are his God-hero. A man walks into church searching for a leader he can look up to and respect. He wants a father who will instruct, encourage, and guide him. He seeks a man who is strong enough to confront him with the truth—in love.

Here's the terrifying part: if a man loves his pastor, he is crazy about his church. But if he dislikes his pastor, he is unhappy with his church. Nothing else seems to matter much.

I often ask men, "What do you think about your church?" They don't talk about the ministries. They don't talk about the facilities.

They don't talk about their friendships. They talk about their pastor. "Oh, Pastor Jimmy is just a regular guy. He's the greatest!" Or, "Our new pastor is a lousy teacher. I'm starving to death."

Dr. Michael Lindsay found the number one reason high-achieving men don't go to church is they don't respect the pastor. Those men who *did* go to church often chose a megachurch because they saw the pastor as their leadership peer. "Respecting the senior pastor is vital to predicting whether a man is actively involved," Lindsay says.[1]

Pastors, you are the single most important factor in your church's ability to reach men. Not what you preach, but who you are. With men, everything else is secondary. Men will choose or reject your church based on their respect for you.

Women are different. They see their church as a network of relationships. If they have friends in the church, the kids are happy in youth group, and the sermons are passable, they are content. Pastoral quality is one of many variables women weigh in evaluating their church. For men, it's the bottom line.

The bad news: this is a lot of pressure on you. The good news: you are in a unique position to reach more men. Here are some practical suggestions to help you connect with guys. I'm going to avoid the obvious suggestions (preach better sermons, don't be hypocritical) and focus on some you may never have considered.

RELATE TO THE MEN

There's a stereotype that pastors and priests are pantywaists. You see this all the time in movies. Cinematic pastors are low-key, avuncular souls who mumble their way through weddings and funerals. They are decidedly less masculine than the hero who's getting married or the mobster who's being buried.

Is there any truth to this? According to personality tests, "men entering the ordained ministry exhibit more 'feminine' personality characteristics than men in the population at large."[2] Think about what the job entails: pastors must be verbal, sensitive, studious, loving, and relational. In other words, ministers must possess the Venus skills we commonly associate with women.

Catholic priests are all male, but they are males who turn their backs on typical manly behavior. They are prohibited from pursuing women, marrying, having sex, raising children, building wealth, and owning property. Jesuit Patrick Arnold writes,

> "Real (spiritual) Men" must abandon most of the values and enterprises nearest to men's hearts—competition, fighting, sexual expressiveness, generativity, economic productivity, adventure, autonomy—in favor of a eunuch's existence. The eunuch motif is even present in the premier model held up to married Christian men: Joseph the husband of Mary, usually presented as an old man, sexless and frozen ideal. It is little wonder that so many men get a strong unconscious message that involvement with Christian spirituality requires a kind of emasculation. It seems to them that the men best suited for Christian life are odd and asexual, nerds, or very old and "out of gas."[3]

Men respect pastors who are properly masculine. They are drawn to men who, like Jesus, embody both lion and lamb. They find macho men and sissies equally repulsive.

MEN WANT A PASTOR WHO'S A REGULAR GUY

Lee Strobel says unchurched men "prefer down-to-earth, straight talking leaders, ones who don't insist on 'Doctor' or 'Reverend' before their names." Strobel also recommends giving up perks, parking places, even the ministerial robe: "Those trappings smack of elitism and, in some cases, arrogance."[4] Thom Rainer quotes formerly unchurched Larry from Boston, who praises his pastor's authenticity: "Pat is just a real guy. He doesn't try to pretend to be somebody he's not."[5]

A minister who speaks openly of his struggles, failings, and challenges will win points with men. I love it when my pastor stands in the pulpit and admits he is not perfect: "Last night, my wife and I had a fight. Yours truly, Mr. Holiness, was preparing a sermon from God's Word, and I blew it." A dash of humility from the pastor really helps the men relate.

Sometimes this truth-telling can be an emotional experience. You might choke up or even cry in front of the church. Be judicious about emotive displays. Jesus wept publicly, but he did so at the funeral of a friend, an appropriate forum for male grief. Men don't mind an occasional display of genuine emotion from the pastor, but they resist feigned sentiment designed to manipulate the crowd. Men can smell a rat.

MEN LIKE PASTORS WHO HAVE THE TRAPPINGS OF MANHOOD

Jeri Odell's husband, Dean, was impressed with her new pastor because he wore cowboy boots when he preached.[6] Athletes-turned-pastors, such as Robert Lewis and Miles McPherson, are very popular with men. Stu Weber, one of America's leading men's pastors, is a former Green Beret.

Pastor, you don't have to be Arnold Schwarzenegger to attract men, but the more trappings of manhood, the better. Men will judge you by the clothes you wear, the car you drive, and the hobbies you pursue. (Not fair, but it's true.) The more time you spend outdoors, the better. If you were once employed in a field other than ministry, speak of it often, especially if you served in the military or worked in blue-collar fields. By all means, mention your man-stuff from the pulpit. Whenever you shoot skeet, play a round of golf, or enter a bike race, be sure the congregation knows. This is not bragging—you're letting the men know you're one of them.

MEN APPRECIATE CERTITUDE AND CONVICTION

Men want a pastor who is firm in his convictions. Listen to Jorge, a formerly unchurched man: "I visited a few churches before I became a Christian. Man, some of them made me want to vomit! They didn't show any more conviction about their beliefs than I did." Sean's resistance to church softened after hearing a pastor who preached with certitude: "The first time I heard him, I thought, *This guy really believes this stuff.* I guess I really surprised Marilyn when I told her I wanted to go back for another visit."

Men want a pastor who proclaims the gospel with boldness, unashamedly and unapologetically, but not with a condemnation or guilt. Thom Rainer asked the formerly unchurched what they liked in a pastor, and he reported, "Numerous times we heard how these pastors were strong in their convictions but gentle in spirit."[7]

AVOID PREACHER-SPEAK

Certain Christian traditions encourage preachers to talk differently when they preach and pray aloud. This is called *ministerial tone.* Seminaries discourage it, but some Christians insist on it. The moment the pastor enters the pulpit, he's expected to change his speaking cadence and accent. For example, Southern preachers are renowned for calling on the name of JAY-sus or ending sentences with an uplifted, "Amen!" Other pastors do a lot of whoopin' and hollerin' or adopt a singsong tone in the pulpit. Mainline pastors sometimes adopt a highbrow ministerial tone, draaaaagging out their voooooowels, speaking slooowly and distinctly. Once the sermon is over, the pastor speaks normally again.

The problem with preacher-speak is that men may see it as performance, not heartfelt communication. Your message may be obscured because the listener is paying attention to the way you speak and not to the words you're speaking. Make your preaching delivery as conversational as possible. Passion in the pulpit is great, but avoid anything that looks staged or performed.

LEARN TO REALLY LOVE YOUR MEN

Some pastors are uncomfortable in the presence of men. I once heard a minister tell this brutally honest story about his struggle to love his men. Here's my paraphrased version:

I was a bookish kid with skinny arms and thick glasses. When I entered junior high, the big, athletic boys started picking on me—calling me "faggot" and "mama's boy" and slamming me into lockers. I hated this bullying and learned to avoid the jocks through high school.

In college, I heard a call to ministry. I discovered a deep love for the Scriptures. I went on to seminary and became a pastor.

My first church was a small, rural congregation full of old people. I took to my role with gusto. Life was good as my bride and I settled into our roles.

One Sunday, something unexpected happened: a power couple in their late twenties walked into the church. She was petite and beautiful, and he was . . . a jock. Broad shoulders. Prominent brow. Large fists.

I could hardly get through my sermon that day. By the time I delivered the benediction I was an emotional wreck—but I had no idea why.

The following week, the power couple showed up in the adult Sunday school class, which I led. I stammered through my lesson, and then opened it up for discussion. The jock opened his mouth and offered a brash opinion that contradicted Scripture. I felt a rush of pleasure as I corrected his theology. My tone was harsh and condescending. We never saw the couple again.

Years later, I was hired by a larger church. It had a men's ministry program. The guys always invited me to participate, but I was so busy in my new job I never seemed to have the time.

One day Elmer, one of our elders and a leader in the men's ministry, made an offhand comment that brought me to my knees. He said to me, "Pastor, why don't we see you at our men's gatherings? Are you afraid of men?"

Elmer had hit the bull's-eye. In a moment of shining clarity, I saw myself slammed against a locker. My survival strategy since junior high was to avoid men—particularly masculine ones. In fact, by going into the ministry, I had chosen a career that kept me away from manly things altogether. Eighty percent of my daily interactions were with women—and I liked it that way. In those rare instances when I had to deal with men, there was usually a woman present, which kept me safe.

When I was a boy, I was powerless against the jocks. But now the tables were turned. As a pastor, I had the power. My weapon was my doctor of theology, and I used it like a club to bludgeon my adversaries and have my revenge.

I prayed and asked God's forgiveness. I asked him to give me a real love for men—even the big, scary ones.

So I attended my first men's breakfast. I started mentoring a group of young men. I told my story to other pastors. One Sunday I even wore shoulder pads and a football jersey in the pulpit as an illustration.

To my delight, when I began investing in my men, my heart changed. And so did my church. We started growing. A lot of the gossip and backbiting went away. Even the youth group grew. Young men started sitting in the front row.

I entered the pastorate to protect myself from men, but now I can't imagine doing ministry without them. They are no longer my adversaries—they are my brothers.

If a man wounded you at some point, you may bring a fear of men into your ministry. You may be cool to men, or find yourself competing with them. You may allow yourself to be cowed by an aggressive parishioner—or suddenly lash out in anger at him. You may have an instinctive negative reaction to men's things (hunting, fishing, the military, sports, resource development, muscle cars) that you can't explain.

If any of these describes you, I strongly encourage you to share your story with a small group or a professional counselor. You need healing. Ask God to give you a genuine love for the men in your congregation.

o   o   o

If Moses and Elijah and Paul and Jesus had men in their lives, how much more do you need men at your side? The pastors who stumble are those who walk without brothers. If your church has a men's ministry, get involved. If not, start meeting regularly with a few other men. Your men need you. And you need your men.

Chapter 18

TEACHING AND MEN

PASTOR PHIL DELIVERED A GOOD MESSAGE. IT WAS INTERESTING, theologically sound, and well buttressed with Scripture. At thirty-two minutes it got the congregation out in time to beat the Baptists to the restaurants.

That evening at the business meeting, Pastor Phil opened with prayer and then asked the elders which of his three main points they thought was best. Not one of them could remember anything he'd said. The elders were embarrassed. Phil was discouraged.

There's a lot of teaching going on in church, but not much learning. These days the gospel is not so much falling on deaf ears—it's bouncing off of overloaded brains.

Travel back with me to 1875. There was no radio, TV, or Internet. Common folks lived on far-flung farms and rarely saw a newspaper. The sermon was the only new idea they heard all week. They'd talk about it in the wagon on the way home and think about it for six days as they threw their backs into mundane chores.

Too many preachers and teachers still communicate as if it's 1875. They assume people are absorbing what they say. But the church lost its communication monopoly decades ago. It sounds so spiritual to say, "Well, I'll just preach God's Word and leave the results to him. I know his Word won't return void."

Reality check: the vast majority of Christian teaching today returns void. The church is one of many voices screaming for people's attention. These days a man can flip out his smartphone and watch TV, check his messages, or play a game right in the middle of a worship service. I've seen it. Teachers, you are now competing for people's attention *inside* the church—during your message. You must become a more effective communicator.

Christ showed us how to impart the gospel with effectiveness and power. Here are some strategies Jesus used to reach men.

BEFORE YOU TEACH . . .

Thomas Edison said, "Success is 10 percent inspiration and 90 percent perspiration." Effective teachers put in the hard work before they begin.

Be Prepared

Jesus knew his subject. The Bible says, "He taught them as one having authority."[1]

Before you teach or preach, be prepared. Read up. Study. Most important, outline your message. There's power in a well-organized presentation. Also, make sure your topic is relevant to your audience. Men love truth they can use; they have little interest in Bible trivia.

Gather Great Stories

Christ was first and foremost a storyteller. His parables are the most famous body of teaching in the world.

One time I was talking to a veteran preacher. He was a master communicator who had built a large church. I asked him what his secret of successful communication was. "It's simple," he said. "Great illustrations. I know people aren't going to remember what I say. But all week they'll remember the stories, the object lessons, and the anecdotes I bring to the pulpit. Illustrations and object lessons are like little robots that keep working in people's lives long after I say amen."

Prepare Object Lessons

Many of Christ's parables were object lessons. Christ took something at hand—a coin, a sheep, a wineskin—and built an unforgettable lesson around it.

Years ago at a men's event, our pastor used water and a copper pipe to illustrate how men are to be conduits of God's blessing to the people around them. He sent each man home with an inch-long copper tube to put on his keychain. I still see copper tubes whenever my friends pull out their keys. I ask them what it means, pretending not to know. The men quickly explain the illustration to me. Needless to say, this lesson has had a lasting impact on the men of our church.

Pastor, bring an object lesson into the pulpit every week. Within three years you'll have a church full of men.

Gather Visuals

Using visuals has gotten a lot easier in the twenty-first century. With modern projection systems and the Internet, you have millions of still images and libraries of professionally produced video clips at your disposal.

Say you're telling a story about William Shakespeare. Pop an image of the Bard up on the big screen. Comparing apples to oranges? Project an image of both. Men remember what they see more than what they hear.

More powerful are high-quality, custom-made videos from websites such as SermonSpice.com and BluefishTV.com. MovieMinistry .com provides prebuilt sermon illustrations using film clips from hundreds of popular movies. Content is searchable by keyword and topic. Visual content is cheap to buy, easy to use, and compelling to men.

Above all, don't just pop PowerPoint text bullets up on the screen. Men do not remember words—they remember images.

WHEN YOU TEACH . . .

How you teach may be just as important as what you teach. The next time you instruct men, try these ideas:

Keep It Short

One time I was stuck on a long cross-country flight. I had my Bible and some time to kill. I happened to have with me a list of the parables of Jesus. So I timed each one with a stopwatch. Then I took an average. Go ahead; take a guess: How long do you think it takes to preach the average parable of Jesus?

Thirty-eight seconds.

The lessons that changed the course of history comfortably preach in under a minute.[2]

That day, while I sat cruising at thirty-five thousand feet, God showed me a simple truth: it is not the length of your teaching but its impact that changes men's hearts.

All things being equal, shorter is better for men. Lengthy sermons and lessons are generally a turn-off for guys. (African-American churches, known for three-hour worship services and ninety-minute sermons, suffer the largest gender gaps.) Never mind that pastors like Mark Driscoll preach an hour. Verily I say unto you, few pastors have the chops to keep a modern audience's attention for sixty minutes. If Jesus clocked in at thirty-eight seconds, what makes you think you need an hour or more?

It's been said that a good sermon is like a good skirt: long enough to cover the essentials, but short enough to keep you interested. Even a boring preacher can keep his audience's attention if he's brief. (I know *you* are never boring. I'm talking to the other guys.) Don't wander here and there—get to the point and toss everything that doesn't relate to the point. If you have more to say than can be said in a few minutes, break your teaching into shorter segments. This is how I teach at men's retreats: I speak for ten minutes, and then I allow the men to discuss for ten minutes. Men love this format.

Use Humor and Laughter

Jesus laughed. No joke.[3]

The most effective teachers sprinkle their talks with humor—particularly as they begin. Why? Because when a man laughs, he drops his guard. Laughing changes a man from a detached listener into a participator. And men love to laugh. They are the primary viewers of the Comedy Central cable channel, and they are the biggest fans of late-night TV comedians. A church that is full of laughter and fun will soon find itself full of men—and young people too.

Start with Real Life

Robert Lewis's approach to teaching men is simple: "You don't teach the Bible first. You teach real life issues first; then you bring the Bible in to surprise them. Most men's ministries fail because they are Bible studies. I always start with the practical and bring the Bible in on the back end."[4] Lewis sums up his approach this way: give men what they need, disguised as what they want. Wasn't this Jesus' method? The woman at the well wanted a drink, but she needed abundant life. Jesus offered her living water. He framed the gospel to reflect her desire.

Do Something Unexpected

The Bible says of Jesus: "the people were astonished at His teaching."[5] When was the last time you were astonished in church? Men need to be amazed by God, but our liturgies and rituals have made him utterly predictable. No wonder men find church so boring. My advice: when teaching men, do the unexpected. Break something. Pretend something's going wrong. Do a card trick. Take them outside. Light something on fire (besides a candle). Challenge a cherished assumption. Arrange for a critic to stand up and argue with you—right in the middle of the sermon. Get off the stage and wander the aisles while you preach. Astonish men, and watch them lock in.

Make It Challenging

Robert Lewis tells the story of a rough-and-tumble construction worker who approached him after a Men's Fraternity meeting. He stuck out a calloused hand and said, "Man, every time I come in here, you just crush my toes. You're just livin' in my jock shorts.

Everything you talk about is right where I live."⁶ Generally speaking, the more frank and hard-hitting the teaching, the more men like it— as long as it doesn't stray into condemnation or moralism.

Jesus' teaching was so electric because it challenged the status quo. One of his favorite phrases was, "You've heard that it was said . . . but I say to you . . ." Speaking personally, there's nothing better than a lesson that challenges my assumptions and spurs me to action. And there's nothing worse than a pabulum sermon of familiar truths I've heard a thousand times.

Many teachers feel that every word out of a Christian's mouth must be sweet as honey, carefully considered so that no one's feelings are bruised. But men appreciate forthrightness and honesty. They respect a teacher who tells it like it is and doesn't beat around the bush. Teach as Jesus did: be direct—and get to the point.

Emphasize Strength More than Weakness

My church in Alaska used to have an associate pastor who was really into therapy. His messages were all about brokenness, weakness, unworthiness, and dependence on God. Although men need to acknowledge their brokenness, they don't need to wallow in it. The words *strong* and *strength* appear 561 times in the New King James Version, while *weak* and *weakness* show up just 83 times. It's far more effective to speak of strength when teaching men.

Use Masculine Imagery and Language

I picked up a recruiting brochure for the US Army the other day. Bold letters on the front cover invited me to "Rise to the Challenge." As you read, notice the masculine imagery and language:

> If you're looking for a job that will challenge you from day one, look no further than the U.S. Army. As a Soldier in the Army of One, you'll engage in life faster and better than most people your age . . . you'll experience things that you never thought possible and go places most people only read about. You'll learn your capabilities, sharpen your skills and then push yourself to the limit on

a daily basis. You'll grow stronger, physically, mentally, and feel a
sense of pride you've never felt before.[7]

This ad copy can teach us a lot about men. Listen to what it
promises: challenge, adventure, increased competence, skill, endur-
ance, strength, and pride. It's competitive: you'll be faster, better, and
stronger than the rest. With such imagery the army attracts sixty to
eighty thousand volunteers each year, most of them male.

Leaven your lessons with stories and metaphors that men can
relate to. Analogies from sports, battle, business, and survival capture men's hearts. So does the language of death and sacrifice.

Start and End on Time

So simple, yet so critical. Sometimes things go long in church.
What should you do? Cut a song on the fly. Cut a point from your
sermon. It's usually more important to honor men's time than it is
to "get it all in."

Some churches have no established service length, preferring to
"give the Holy Spirit as much time as he needs." That may sound
spiritual, but churches with wildly varying service length often have
a shortage of men. Start and end on time, and your men will be confident to invite their friends.

TO INVOLVE MEN IN THE LESSON . . .

Most Christian teachers simply stand up and lecture. But the most
effective ones immerse their students in the lesson.

Teach by Personal Experience

Why did Jesus ask Peter to step out of the boat and walk on
water? Peter had heard Jesus' teaching on faith. But that stormy evening, Peter personally discovered what faith really was.

Use active learning techniques whenever possible. Put something in men's hands. Use props, scents, visual aids, anything that
helps men experience the lesson. Why do major corporations spend

millions to send their mostly male executives to play team-building games or walk across hot coals? The lessons that change lives cannot be absorbed from a lecture or book.

In Discussions, Stir the Pot

Men process truth through argumentation and give-and-take. But in the church we strain toward niceness. We are uncomfortable with conflict. We've adopted an eleventh commandment: *if you can't say anything nice, don't say anything at all.*

Is this Christlikeness or cowardice? Jesus was so bold in his arguments with the Pharisees that they often left wanting to kill him. Christ's fiery words embarrassed his own disciples. Even Jesus' friends were burned by his flamethrower tongue.[8]

The next time you're teaching men, ask provocative questions. Stir the pot. Set two rules: (1) nothing's off-limits, and (2) we all walk out of here friends.

Issue a Clear Call to Action

During the Civil War, Abraham Lincoln was known to slip into New York Avenue Presbyterian Church on Wednesday nights to hear the preaching of Rev. Phineas D. Gurley. One evening, as Lincoln and a companion left the church to return to the White House, the companion asked, "What did you think of tonight's sermon?"

Lincoln answered, "It was brilliantly conceived, relevant, and well presented."

"So it was a great sermon," the companion said.

"No, it failed," Lincoln replied. "It failed because Dr. Gurley did not ask anything great of us."

Men give up their weekends to come to church. You'd better tell them why they came. Don't be afraid to ask something great of them. Give the men a specific assignment for the week. Call it "The Pastor's Challenge." Not all the men will take the challenge, but 100 percent participation is not the point. You've set the expectation that men do something with what they've heard.

I know a number of smaller churches that call men ages eighteen and older forward at the end of the service for "The Men's Huddle." The pastor shares a two-minute object lesson that cements his message in their minds. And he passes out a "touchstone," a small object that men carry in their pockets all week to remind them of the message.

When the man returns to his family, the children ask, "What did you get, Daddy?" He produces the touchstone and explains the lesson to his children. For the first time in his life, a regular Joe can be a spiritual leader in his home—because his pastor equipped him. (To learn more about the men's huddle and other teaching ideas, visit my website, www.churchformen.com.)

o   o   o

Jesus taught for the male brain, and everyone marveled at his teaching. As you prepare for your next class, remember to keep it concise, visual, and interactive. Follow his example, and you'll draw men to him.

Chapter 19

GETTING THE BIG
STORY RIGHT

I'VE SEEN MY FAVORITE MOVIE AT LEAST TWO HUNDRED TIMES.
Let me tell you about it.

It stars a handsome man who's extremely dangerous. He holds
the power of life and death in his bare hands. He's amazingly skilled
at everything. He speaks many languages. He never panics. He's
always in control.

Our hero is given an impossible assignment. He must go undercover to defeat a well-armed, murderous enemy single-handedly. If
he fails, the world as we know it will come to an end. Calamity will
strike. Millions will die.

Almost immediately things go wrong. His allies betray him.
Suddenly he's an outlaw. Both the good guys *and* the bad guys are hunting him down. Still, he must complete his mission. Lives are at stake.

He falls into his enemy's hands. He endures a brutal beating
that would land any other man in the ICU. However, through a
mixture of strength and cunning, our hero escapes his captor. He
pulls off a series of miraculous exploits and completes his mission in
the most unexpected fashion. As a bonus, he wins the affections of
a beautiful woman.

Men the world over love this movie. They pay big bucks to see it
again and again. Sometimes the hero goes by the name of Bond—James

Bond. Other times he's named Ethan Hunt, Jason Bourne, Frodo, Neo, Eli, Superman, or Spider-Man. Though the plot twists vary from film to film, the big story remains the same.

o o o

Why do men love this movie? It's a reflection of the big story that's written on the heart of every man. Want to know a secret? Every man longs for a hero—and to be one himself.

Want to know another secret? This big story is simply a retelling of the Gospels.

Consider the parallels. Christ came to earth as a dangerous man—skilled, knowledgeable, and in control. He held the power of life and death in his hands. He was given an impossible assignment—to overcome a ruthless enemy single-handedly. He preferred to work undercover and told people not to reveal his secrets. His life involved a series of miraculous exploits. He was betrayed by an ally and handed over to his enemy, whose henchmen beat him almost beyond recognition. Yet he miraculously escaped his captors and completed his mission in the most unexpected fashion. He slipped the bonds of death and defeated his murderous enemy. The world was saved. In the end, he will receive a radiant bride.

The story written on the hearts of men is the story of Jesus. But few men realize it. They go to the multiplex to catch a glimpse of the divine, when they could find the real thing in a local church.

So who's actually sitting in church, getting the mission briefing? For the most part, it's women, children, and elderly men. Where are the action-oriented guys? They're out doing action-oriented things. Or they're sitting in the dark, eating popcorn, watching a Jesus stand-in save the world against impossible odds.

Yes, there are some action-oriented guys who go to church—and thank God for them. If only there were more. But imagine the power our congregations would have if there were a few more James Bonds among us.

So how do we get high-powered risk takers to come to church?

How can you encourage men to become the heroes God wants them to be? How can we train young Spider-Men in the making?

We have to get the big story right. The gospel is about a courageous man whose mission is to save the world—a man who is currently recruiting agents to assist him in this work. But during the twentieth century, the big story changed in our churches. Allow me to demonstrate.

In chapter 12, I pointed out a phrase that is never mentioned in the Bible, yet somehow has become the number one way evangelicals describe discipleship. The phrase is, *a personal relationship with Jesus Christ.*

When Christ called disciples, he did not say, "Come, have a personal relationship with me." No, he simply said, "Follow me." Hear the difference? *Follow me* suggests a mission. A goal. But *a personal relationship with Jesus* suggests we're headed to Starbucks for some couple time.

This subtle change in how we describe the gospel is one of the reasons our message becomes garbled on its way to the masculine soul. Presenting the gospel as a relationship does not point a man toward the big story that's written on his heart. Let me show you what it does point to.

o o o

My wife also has a favorite movie that she's seen at least five hundred times.

The film stars an attractive, young, single woman who lives in an exotic locale. She wears fabulous clothes and has an amazing home (often a loft apartment in New York). She's smart, sexy, and busy. Too busy for a man.

Then *he* shows up. At first she hates him. He's loud, obnoxious . . . and undeniably attractive. Through a series of misadventures (usually involving water), fate brings them together.

He woos her. At first she resists, but eventually her heart melts, and they fall in love. They live happily ever after.

If you haven't seen where I'm going yet, let me connect the dots.

Men's movies: a hero saves the world against impossible odds.

Women's movies: a woman finds a happy relationship with a wonderful man.

In today's church, the gospel is no longer about saving the world against impossible odds. It's about finding a happy relationship with a wonderful man.

If the point of going to church is to pursue a relationship, you will draw more women than men. *The End*. Roll credits.

This point is so important I must say it again: if we're going to transform men from passive pew-sitters into battle-ready warriors, we must get the big story right. The gospel is the story of a courageous man who is out to save the world against impossible odds. And he is recruiting agents to join him. He is calling you to risk everything to come under his command. And when the mission is over, a precious reward awaits. That's the message men crave. It's a message that's lost in today's therapeutic church.

How do we get this message out to men without scaring the ladies? Try these ideas.

PROMISE RISK

Whenever Ethan Hunt, the hero of the Mission Impossible films, receives his briefing, the risks are clear. The recording always ends like this: "Your mission, *should you decide to accept it . . .*" Hunt's assignments are so demanding he's always given a chance to pass.

He never does.

We would be wise to promise more risk to men in church. Do me a favor. Put this book down, grab your Bible, and read Matthew 10:16–30. This is where Jesus presents his mission briefing to the disciples. Go ahead and read it. I'll wait.

Okay. What did you think? Christ obviously flunked Church Recruiting 101. I've seen a lot of Christian promotional materials, but never one that mentions the possibility of death, injury, or loss. Can you imagine a pastor greeting the new members' class this way:

"Welcome to Sunnyside Church. Join us every Sunday for flogging, betrayal, persecution, and death."

Why would Christ psych out his own team right before kickoff?

Jesus knew men. There's a certain type of man who will not give his all unless he sees danger on the horizon. But our churches are such safe, predictable places, this kind of man does not invest himself. Instead, he takes his risks elsewhere, devoting his best efforts to building earthly kingdoms.

My home state of Alaska is full of such men. These guys don't vacation on a beach in Hawaii; they risk life and limb to go mountain sheep hunting. They spend a small fortune to fly in tiny planes to big mountains where the trophy sheep are. These men climb sheer cliff faces in the spitting snow, battling hypothermia, hunger, and injury. One misstep could send them plunging to their deaths. In fact, a handful of hunters perish every autumn in Alaska. These high-octane men wouldn't have it any other way. They appreciate the nearly impossible challenge that sheep hunting provides. Overcoming obstacles is just part of the fun.

Antarctic explorer Ernest Shackleton was looking for this kind of man when he posted this advertisement in 1913:

> Men wanted for hazardous journey. Small wages. Bitter cold. Long months of complete darkness. Constant danger. Safe return doubtful. Honour and recognition in case of success.

More than five thousand men applied for twenty-six slots. Precisely the kind of men who are missing in today's church. If we want men who will penetrate the culture with the gospel, we must do what Jesus did and promise suffering, trial, and pain. But today's Christianity is marketed like Tylenol: it's the antidote to suffering, trial, and pain. We've turned Jesus' approach on its head.

Now here's a strategy you probably never learned in evangelism training: it's sometimes wise to rebuff a man's first attempt to receive Christ. Certain men need to feel God's rebuke before they will walk at his side.

My friend Paul is such a man. He's one of Alaska's premier bush pilots and the owner of a wilderness lodge. He's an adventurer who's made the first ascent of some of Alaska's toughest peaks. Paul was raised in church by devout parents. But for decades he ran from God, and his life was falling apart. One Sunday he approached a pastor he had known for years and asked how to become a Christian. The wise pastor looked him in the eye and said, "Don't waste my time. When you're ready to give everything to God, come back and see me." He turned and left Paul at the altar, stunned.

Does this sound crazy to you? Look at how Jesus handled a similar encounter: "Along the way someone said to Jesus, 'I'll go anywhere with you!'"[1] And what did Jesus say? "Welcome, my good man. It's so nice to have you in our group. Bartholomew has a new disciple packet and a coffee mug for you."

Not. Here's how Christ actually addressed the potential recruit: "Foxes have dens, and birds have nests, but the Son of Man doesn't have a place to call his own."[2] Modern translation: *Follow me, and you'll be homeless the rest of your life.* In the next four verses Jesus rebuked two other would-be followers, one for wanting to say good-bye to his family, and one for wanting to bury his father. How insensitive.

Yet Christ knew what we have forgotten: a man who is challenged into God's kingdom will be a follower forever. That's what happened with my friend Paul. A few weeks after the pastor rebuffed him, Paul flew his bush plane into Anchorage and gave everything to God. He's been transformed from an unfaithful lout to the world's most doting husband. And he's using his wilderness lodge as a proving ground for young, male disciples.

DON'T BEG OR PLEAD

Jesus never begged anyone to follow him. He never waited for anyone, never sang one more verse while people decided whether to follow. He commanded, "Follow me" and kept going. Those who immediately dropped everything became his disciples; those who hesitated were left behind.

Yet week after week, especially in evangelical churches, we beg men to be saved. Problem is, the call to be saved is so familiar, men see no value in it. Don't misunderstand me: it's vital that we call men to follow Jesus. Men need salvation. But instead of pleading, what if our approach was: "Do you have what it takes to follow Christ? Many say they do, but fewer than one in four will remain loyal. Are you one of the few, or when trials come, will you crumble?"[3] What if we stopped begging men to be saved and started challenging them to follow Jesus Christ?

PROMISE REWARD

Once the mission is over, our cinematic hero always gets his reward (usually the beautiful woman). But in church, we shy away from talking about reward. It seems so selfish. So fleshly. We should do what's right just because it's right. Right?

Return with me to Matthew 10. After Jesus blasts his disciples with predictions of doom, he finishes with the promise of reward.

> He who receives a prophet in the name of a prophet shall receive a prophet's reward. And he who receives a righteous man in the name of a righteous man shall receive a righteous man's reward. And whoever gives one of these little ones only a cup of cold water in the name of a disciple, assuredly, I say to you, he shall by no means lose his reward.[4]

Reward. Reward. Reward. Jesus knows men. And men respond to the promise of reward. This desire is not sin; it's the way God made us.

Flip over to Matthew 19:16–26. Christ encounters a rich young ruler. He's upright, powerful, capable, and wealthy. If I were Jesus, I'd be thinking, *This guy's righteous—and loaded. He could fund my ministry for years. I gotta grab him!* But of course, Jesus does exactly the opposite—he places an obstacle in front of him: "If you want to be perfect, go, sell what you have and give to the poor, and you will have treasure in heaven; and come, follow Me."⁵ He then warns the crowd that it's nearly impossible for a rich person to enter the kingdom of heaven.

Right on the heels of this stunning declaration, the apostle Peter (Mr. Perfect Timing himself) decides to ask Jesus this question: "We have left everything to be your followers! What will we get?"⁶

Uh-oh. Suddenly eleven pairs of eyes are fixed on Peter. I imagine the other disciples swallowed in unison. *Didn't he just hear what Jesus said about riches? The Boss is going to tear him to bits!* Judas probably started taking bets on whether Peter would survive the certain rebuke.

But the reprimand does not come. Instead, Jesus makes an audacious promise of eternal reward:

> Yes, all of you have become my followers. And so in the future world, when the Son of Man sits on his glorious throne, I promise that you will sit on twelve thrones to judge the twelve tribes of Israel. All who have given up home or brothers and sisters or father and mother or children or land for me will be given a hundred times as much. They will also have eternal life. But many who are now first will be last, and many who are last will be first.⁷

Jesus did not shy away from the promise of reward. He did not worry that he might appeal to the flesh. He showed us that it's perfectly healthy to motivate men by helping them understand the rewards they accumulate when they serve the kingdom of God.

Please keep in mind: we are not Jesus. We cannot promise a man a heavenly mansion with an ocean view if he'll volunteer in Sunday school this weekend. Nor do I endorse the manipulative way some televangelists promise reward to those who send money.

Just because some have abused the promise of reward, we cannot ignore it. Risk and reward go hand in hand throughout the New Testament. When we refuse to point men toward eternal rewards, we reject a motivational tool Christ used repeatedly.

o   o   o

Many people think the church asks too much of its members. In reality, it asks too little. Thomas Rainer studied two thousand churches and found that without exception, the churches that attracted irreligious people were *high-expectation* churches.[8] Dr. Chris Bader found that "groups that are growing in membership are the ones that require more of their members."[9]

Truth is, the gospel is equal parts demanding mission and personal relationship. But these days we stress the relationship, because we need women to keep the ministry machine going. When we present the gospel as if it's a chick flick, is it any wonder more women stick around to see the movie?

Chapter 20

WHAT ABOUT WOMEN?

ONE OF THE MOST COMMON QUESTIONS I GET AFTER MY SEMINARS is this: What about women? If we make church man-friendly, won't women feel left out, just as the men do now? Will they leave the church?

No. Women will stay. In fact, they will probably like church better—especially the young women. To illustrate, let me tell you a story.

Our local home improvement superstore sponsors Do-It-Herself Workshops on Monday nights. I can just hear the conversation between Sheila and her girlfriends at lunch the next day:

SHEILA. Hey, girls, guess what I did last night? I went to Home Depot and learned how to work a band saw.
SHEILA'S FRIENDS. Oooooh, that's cool.

Now, picture this conversation between Chuck and his buddies:

CHUCK. Hey, guys, guess what I did last night? I went to Hobby Lobby and learned how to make decorative pillow shams.
CHUCK'S FRIENDS. [*Stunned silence*]

Here is an ironclad rule of the genders: Women are fascinated by the things of men. But men are repelled by the things of women.

Men are deeply embarrassed to appear feminine in public. When my wife says to me, "Hold my purse for a minute," I'm mortified. I don't want to be seen in public holding a purse. But when I say to my wife, "Hold my hammer for a minute," she feels no shame. Today's women cross over easily into men's roles and do so with delight. Women who conquer traditionally male roles are held up as models. But men are absolutely prohibited from crossing over into women's roles.

This one-way barrier exists at all levels of society. For example, we have tomboys, but no *tomgirls*. Women are flooding into male-dominated careers, but men don't even try for so-called women's jobs—even those that pay well. For example, almost half of the doctors in the United States are women, but only 6 percent of America's nurses are men.[1]

So if a Christian organization presents the gospel in a masculine context, who will be attracted? Women. Men. Children. If it presents that same gospel in a feminine context, who will be attracted? Ladies.

This is why churches that create a healthy masculine environment do not become heavily male. Women do masculine, but men don't do feminine.

I had the pleasure of interviewing several women who attend Christ's Church of the Valley, a megachurch in Phoenix that targets men. Many echoed the comments of Darlene, who said, "In our last church my husband went to church, but he was reluctant. Now he's excited to come. His life is changing, and that's changing our whole family. I can't tell you the difference it's made." Twenty-seven-year-old Trina says, "We [the women] realize this church is about men, and we don't mind it. We like all the guy-oriented stuff."

o   o   o

Back in the 1950s Carl Dudley was pastoring his first church. It wasn't long before he got a visit from the president of the women's association, who informed him, "Men sit on boards, but women run the church." Dudley notes:

Although women held less prestigious positions or none at all, they were not without clout. They remained essential to the strength of the congregation by raising most of the money and providing much of the "manpower" (as it was called) to keep everything running, including the Sunday school, choir, prayer groups and service societies. And they retained what one woman called a "velvet veto" over expenses and programs of which they did not approve.[2]

Women still wield the velvet veto today, and they often use it to drive the masculine spirit out of the church, without even realizing it.

Example 1: Lakeview Baptist Church is a typical graying congregation, caught in a slow decline. Church leaders are considering a name change to Lakeview Christian Fellowship. They're following the lead of thousands of other churches that have attracted new blood by simply dropping their denominational name from the church sign. Lakeview will remain a Baptist church, but it will not trumpet that affiliation.

It seems like a simple change. The reason has been well explained. Everyone agrees the church needs to do something to reverse its fall. But there is opposition nonetheless. Battle lines are drawn. People are divided. Feelings are hurt.

Once the women of the church see the conflict the name change has stirred up, they begin withdrawing their support. They go to the pastor and exercise their velvet veto. The church continues to be known as Lakeview Baptist Church. Peace is restored. And the congregation continues a slow march to its death.

Example 2: Eric planned a night of paintball for the church's fledgling men's group. But two prominent women heard about it and complained to the pastor. "How is paintball remotely Christian?" asked one woman. "Guns are incompatible with the gospel," said another. "What message are we sending to our boys?" The pastor knew a time bomb when he saw it. He asked Eric to find something else for the men to do. They met at the church and studied 1 Timothy. Another men's ministry is neutered.

It doesn't have to be like this. Women, you can use your influence to say yes to the masculine spirit. Let change happen, even that which causes people to grieve. Allow the men to govern themselves. And lend your support to a man-friendly culture in your church. Here are some ideas.

CONSIDER MEN'S NEEDS WHEN PLANNING

Women do a lot of planning in the church, so naturally, they tend to create based on their own needs and expectations. They ask questions like these: "Are we being sensitive enough? Caring enough? Will everyone feel loved and affirmed?" Rarely do women consider men's needs when planning: "Is it visual enough? Are there opportunities to stand up and move around? Can we skip the praise singing at this event?"

Next time you're at a planning meeting, ask yourself: How will the men respond to this? Does this do a good job of meeting the needs and expectations of our men? Is this something a young man would attend?

LET MEN GATHER WITHOUT WOMEN AROUND

One time I was coordinating a men's service day at our church. The idea was to mobilize the men to prepare the building and grounds for an Alaska winter and to perform minor car repairs for people in need. The preparations were moving forward smoothly—until a woman named Nora approached me and said she felt discriminated against. Nora felt she had every right to serve alongside the men. She threatened to go to the elders and ask that the event be canceled if women were not allowed to volunteer.

Did Nora have the right to participate? Absolutely. But I asked her to lay down that right, as a gift to the men. I pointed out that our church had a number of women-only opportunities, but this was the only men's event of the year.

Nora graciously gave up her crusade. The volunteer corps remained man-only and attracted a large crowd of guys, many of whom were the nonreligious husbands of churchgoing wives. I'm convinced the man-only designation helped swell our ranks, and it drew men on the fringe to serve.

Relinquish Control of the Spiritual Portfolio

If you are a strong-willed woman who compels her husband, brother, or adult son to go to church, I ask you to reconsider. Jesus never forced anyone to follow him. You may be driving your man away from God even as you drag him into the sanctuary. There is no benefit to having a man's body in church if his heart is elsewhere.

Maybe all it would take to get your husband/father/son to go to church is to suggest that he choose the church. Then it's no longer your thing; it's his thing. Would you be willing to switch if another church met your man's needs?

Sam Keen observes, "It's a lot easier to be a saint than to live with one."[3] If you are strictly religious but the men in your life are not, you may actually make Christianity more attractive by lightening up a bit. Ask a friend how you might be less religious and more real.

Step Back and Let Men Lead

One time I was speaking to an experienced pastor about the problem of passive men. "Men don't volunteer in church because they know eventually a woman will step forward and take care of it," he said.

How true. All men have a disease. It's called *she'll-take-care-of-it-itis*. It's a form of amnesia. Once a woman starts taking care of something, men forget completely about it.

If you want men involved in your church, recruit them to lead. Set aside leadership positions for laymen. Sounds chauvinistic until you consider that men are heavily outnumbered at church. Think of it as an affirmative action program for Christianity's largest minority group.

Do Not Belittle Men or Act Spiritually Superior

Some women have noticed their spiritual superiority and lord it over men. One time I was attending a couples' Bible study. The leader asked Eduardo to look up a passage in the book of Zephaniah. He searched for a minute or two and finally found Zechariah. In his confusion Eduardo read the wrong verse. His wife, Rita, reached over and grabbed the Bible with a dramatic sigh. She found the passage in about ten seconds and, with a look of triumph, handed the Bible back to her husband. Guess where Eduardo was next week? Not at Bible study; that's for sure.

I've also heard women ridicule and patronize men, saying things like, "You boys go off and have your little retreat; do your men's thing out in the woods." Questioning a man's competence or manhood is not the way to draw him to Christ.

The Impact of Female Clergy

Since the 1950s and '60s, a number of denominations have opened their formal leadership posts to women. This has sparked debate on the question of female leadership in the church. In one camp are the egalitarians who believe that anyone, male or female, should be allowed to assume any position in the church. In the other camp are the complementarians who believe that, while men and women are equal, God has assigned them different roles.

I'm no theologian, so I will not presume to speak for God in this matter. However, statistics indicate that denominations that have opened their doors widest to female leadership are generally declining in membership. Meanwhile, those old-fashioned male-elder-governed churches are holding their own. The "100 Largest and Fastest Growing Churches in America," compiled by *Outreach* magazine, all have a man at the helm.[4]

Meanwhile, America's seminaries are building an army of female pastors. Women are being ordained to the clergy in unprecedented numbers.[5] Mainline Protestant seminaries now admit about as many women as men, and overall, more than a third of divinity students are female, a number that has been rising steadily since the 1970s.[6] If current trends continue, women will eventually dominate the clergy, just as they have every other aspect of church life in America. Dr. Leon Podles predicts, "The Protestant clergy will be a characteristically female occupation, like nursing, within a generation."[7]

The Church of England may have already reached the tipping point. In 1994, the church welcomed its first female priests. Ten years later, the church ordained more women than men—a first for any denominational group. Over the same period, the female-male church attendance ratio went from 55–45 to 63–37.[8] The Church of England is quickly becoming a church of women, by women, and for women.

It's not uncommon today in mainline churches for women to lead the entire service: a female pastor, liturgist, and choir director officiate, while laywomen lead the prayers, serve Communion, and take the offering.

When weeks pass between man-sightings, the brethren begin to lose heart. Soon you can't get the men to do anything. Men defect to other churches or drop out entirely.

I'm not playing a blame game—just stating the facts. Eighty-seven percent of churches with a female senior pastor suffer a man shortage.[9] Female pastors face significant challenges retaining and motivating male parishioners. Among these are:

Softness

Generally, women are more tender and compassionate than men. A female pastor may inadvertently create a more feminine church just by being who she is. Pastors of both genders believe female ministers "are more caring than men about the individual lives of members of the congregation, more pastorally sensitive, more nurturing."[10]

Lack of Example to the Boys

With a male pastor, there's at least one man in the church who's left everything to follow Christ. It's now possible for a boy to grow up in church without ever seeing a man truly living his faith. This could make it even tougher to transmit Christianity to our sons, and lead to enormous gender gaps in the future.

Liberal Views

Female clergy are overwhelmingly liberal, while men tend to hold more conservative views. Fifty-six percent identify themselves as strong feminists compared to 24 percent of male pastors in the same denominations. The top four priorities of female ministers are "economics and social welfare, tolerance and rights, civility, and gay rights."[11]

◦ ◦ ◦

Ready or not, female pastors are coming. Women pastors, teachers, and lay leaders, I entreat you: become students of men. Learn their needs and expectations. Teach the Bible. And present the Lion of Judah as well as the Lamb of God. If you make the church a more comforting, nurturing place, where the top priority is making everyone feel loved and accepted, your church will stagnate.

Can a female pastor reach men? The surprising answer to that question lies in chapter 25.

Chapter 21

YOUNG MEN AND FAITH

IN CHAPTER 14 WE EXAMINED THE MANY REASONS MORE THAN 70 percent of boys who are raised in church abandon it during their teens and twenties. The male religious life cycle looks something like this:

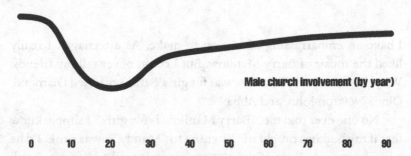

Male church involvement (by year)

0   10   20   30   40   50   60   70   80   90

Little boys attend church without complaint. But sometime around age ten, they begin dropping out. During the late teens and early twenties, male church involvement reaches rock bottom. As men date and marry in their late twenties and thirties, some return, dragged by girlfriends and wives. Others return for the religious instruction of their children. Male involvement grows slowly as men near death.

It's maddening. Young men abandon the faith just as they need the wisdom of Scripture most. Teen boys are forming opinions, lifestyles, and habits that will accompany them their entire lives. It's also a loss for the church, which badly needs young men's energy and drive.

Male church involvement moves exactly opposite of a man's need to be perceived by his peers as manly:

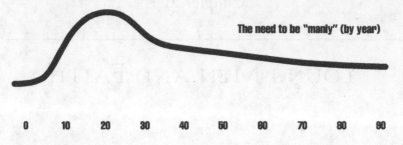

The need to be "manly" (by year)

0   10   20   30   40   50   60   70   80   90

Men are least religious when their need to be manly is greatest. On the other hand, men are more often found in church when their need to prove manhood is weakest—in childhood and old age.

o o o

I have an embarrassing admission to make. As a teenager, I really liked the music of Barry Manilow. But I could never tell my friends. Why? Because Barry Manilow was for girls. Same with Neil Diamond, Olivia Newton-John, and Abba.

No one ever told me, "Barry Manilow is for girls." I simply knew that if my buddies caught me listening to "Mandy," I was sunk. I'd be a laughingstock. Boys of the 1970s were supposed to listen to hard-edged rockers like Led Zeppelin, the Who, and Bachman-Turner Overdrive.

No one ever tells men, "Church is for girls." Young men don't consciously think, *I need to avoid church because my buddies will think I'm less of a man.* But they know that if word gets around that they love Jesus, they'll be sunk.

So they build barriers. They make excuses. They ridicule the church. They dismiss churchgoing men as "religious fanatics" and "mama's boys." Or they keep their faith to themselves.

Other religions recognize the tendency of young men to stray and have built elaborate rituals to keep them engaged. Asian Buddhists train every willing boy to become a novice monk. Jews welcome men through the bar mitzvah. Mormons send their young men on a two-year mission. And tribal religions subject adolescent boys to painful, frightening manhood initiations that most Westerners would condemn as abuse.

And in Christianity we have . . . the confirmation class. Wow. That'll have the boys lining up.

Since the church is unwilling to initiate young men into manhood, they do it themselves. They subject their bodies to all sorts of abuse. They adopt a hypermasculine persona, expunging every trace of femininity. They endure humbling rites of passage: drugs, promiscuity, tattoos, foul language, drunkenness, reckless driving, and violent behavior, to ease their pain and prove their manliness at the same time. And they flee the church, because of its feminine ways and reputation as a place of safety.

What about the "good boys" who don't get into much trouble? Even they prefer manly things. They listen to music that glorifies violence, misogyny, and sex. They play savage video games and gravitate to brutal "cage fighter"–type sports. They watch action movies replete with fights, explosions, and swaggering heroes. Even nerds know that girls go for guys with great skills—nunchuk skills, bow-hunting skills . . . you get the picture.

If Christians could just figure out a way to keep boys engaged in the church, everyone would win. Young men would enter adulthood with fewer addictions, diseases, injuries, and psychological scars. Society would benefit from lower crime rates. And the church would benefit from the vitality young men bring to an organization.

There is a way. It's called *men*.

o o o

Researchers Paul Hill, David Anderson, and Roland Martinson interviewed eighty-eight young men to identify the key relationships through which faith is imparted. Here's what they found:

Relationship That Influenced Men's Faith	No. of Men Who Mentioned This
Family of origin	42
Male mentors	32
Friends	24
Marriage (out of 29 married men)	23
Fathers	21
Extended family	19
Acquaintances	14
Mothers	11

Note how often the Christian faith passes from man to man. Male mentors, friends, and fathers appear high on the list.

What's the old saying? The Christian faith is more caught than taught. Christianity has always passed virally from one man to another. Why do you think Jesus personally discipled twelve men? Or consider the example of Paul, who always took a Barnabas, Silas, or Timothy along on his many journeys. Moses mentored Joshua; Elijah mentored Elisha. Man-to-younger-man is the essential relationship through which courageous faith flows.

But this essential relationship is under a diabolical attack. The recent "pedophile priest" scandals have cast a pall of suspicion over churchmen who want to spend time with boys. A report from the US Conference of Catholic Bishops admits that four out of five abuse victims were teenage boys, and "the crisis was characterized by homosexual behavior."[1]

Today, men are shrinking back from working with youth for fear of being seen as a pervert—or being falsely accused. Society is becoming suspicious of the man-boy relationship—particularly in a religious context. Nonbelieving fathers can now say to themselves, "I'm noble for keeping my son out of church. I wouldn't want him to be abused."

o o o

Researchers from Switzerland examined whether parents' religious habits were transmitted to their offspring. They studied different variables, but one critical factor towered above the rest: the practices of the father determine whether children grow up attending church. And surprisingly, Mom's religiosity has almost no influence over their kids' future devotion.

Consider these findings:

- When Mom is a regular churchgoer but Dad attends infrequently (or never), just 2 to 3 percent of their kids go on to become regular churchgoers.
- When both Mom and Dad attend church regularly, 33 percent of kids grow up as regular attendees.
- Here's the shocker: when Dad is faithful but Mom never attends, 44 percent of the kids end up as regular churchgoers. This is the highest outcome of any scenario.[2]

This study seems to indicate that in spiritual matters, kids take their cues from Dad—at least in Switzerland. But does the pattern hold in the US?

LifeWay Research surveyed more than one thousand adults ages eighteen to thirty who had attended a Protestant church in high school. The study found that 70 percent of these "raised in church" kids stopped attending for at least a year between the ages of eighteen and twenty-two. Researchers studied what caused them to drop out and what factors kept them faithful. And what do you know: those kids whose fathers attended church regularly were much less likely to drop out as young adults. The researchers wrote, "While more mothers attend church, the father's attendance makes a bigger impact on [a young person's] decision to stay in church."[3]

Curtis Burnam, a twenty-five-year veteran of youth ministry, identifies a clear relationship between a dad's participation in church and his children's participation in youth group. "Kids who are taken to church by Mom but not Dad are harder to keep in church," he says. "They tend to drop out at higher rates when they reach adolescence. They are also harder to engage when they do come to youth group. This is especially true of boys—but also of girls."

o o o

So what can you do? Let's start with the little boys.

The best thing you can do for your tiger cub is consistently implant the idea that church is a guy thing. You want him to see that men are just as involved in the church as women—or even more so.

For many years, my wife was the de facto spiritual leader in our home—particularly on Sunday morning. She got the kids up for church and kept us on schedule. Like a lot of Christian men, I wasn't too excited about going to church. I think my kids absorbed my attitude, and every one of them withdrew from church for a while during their teens. If I could go back in time, I would get the kids up on Sunday and take them to their Sunday school classes. I would show more enthusiasm, instead of being a fourth kid on Sunday.

But I wasn't a total slouch: I led mealtime prayers and read Bible stories to the kids at bedtime. My wife and I frequently talked about the sermon in the car on the way home from church, and I was not shy to ask for prayer or mention what God was doing in our family. I led the home group ministry in our church as well as our own home group. My kids saw me investing in the kingdom, and I think that's helped draw them back to the faith as they've grown up.

Bottom line: kids (particularly boys) who see their fathers practicing the faith are much more likely to remain faithful as teens and adults.

o o o

Now, about Sunday school . . .

If your church offers traditional, classroom-based Sunday school, you can make it into a boy-friendly experience. Here are some tips:

- Separate the boys from the girls, even if you have to combine grades. Gender identification is more important than age grouping.
- Choose a curriculum that's boy-friendly. I've included a list of these on my website, www.churchformen.com. At least one organization offers curriculum specifically written for boys.
- Boys with poor reading skills dread Sunday school. Please, don't make young men read around the circle—especially if there are girls present.
- Bring an object lesson every week. One clever teacher brought a fresh cow tongue to class when he taught James 3. Any time you send boys home from Sunday school with blood on their hands, you've done your job.

Curt Hammill teaches a third- and fourth-grade boys' Sunday school class at Burke Community Church in Virginia. He doesn't just teach from a book; he involves his boys in the biblical narrative. For example, he once taught his class about Paul's shipwreck in Acts 27 using cargo (empty boxes), masts (poles and sheets), a plastic sword, and a real storm (electric fans and spray bottles). As he read the story, the boys acted out each part, tossing cargo overboard, doing depth soundings, and so on. As the storm intensified, Curt turned up the fans and increased the number of spray bottles.

Another boring Sunday school lesson? No way. The boys exploded from the classroom like a herd of charging buffaloes, cheeks still glistening from "sea spray." They couldn't wait to tell their parents about Paul's shipwreck.

Curt has even figured out a way to get the boys to pray at the end of class. Everyone gets in a circle and puts one hand in the middle, like a pregame football huddle. The boys offer brief prayers; then it's one-two-three *break*! Young guys like praying this way.

Some churches have dropped the classroom model altogether. They're building large, open rooms for children's ministry, and adopting a style that gives boys an equal chance to win.

My church in Alaska is at the forefront of this growing trend. Here's what children's ministry looks like on Sunday mornings in Anchorage:

- We've dropped the name Sunday school. It's called Adventureland.
- As children arrive, they're allowed to run around in a large room with lots of things to play with. One room even has a mini climbing wall.
- After some free play, the kids gather to sing a few fun songs.
- The leader welcomes everyone and transitions into a group game or a competition between two or three kids.
- Next, the lights dim for a professionally produced video that sets up the Bible lesson.
- Once the video wraps up, it's off to small groups by age and gender—boys with male teachers, and girls with female teachers.
- The small group session is a simple, one-point Bible lesson. The leader reads and then asks questions. There might also be an object lesson (cow tongue, anyone?). No one is compelled to read aloud.
- At the end of small group, the youngsters share prayer requests and pray briefly together.
- Then it's time for more free play until the parents show up.

This new children's ministry is fun. It's active. It disadvantages neither gender. Most important, it puts boys with men, so the faith-virus can spread. I believe this model of youth education will pay big dividends for the church of the future. As more boys "win" in Sunday school, we'll see more of them in church as teens. That is, if we start getting youth group right . . .

o   o   o

In chapter 14, I lamented about how youth groups are rapidly attuning to the female heart. They're becoming more emotive, more verbal, and way more musical. This model is great for girls, and for the boys who happen to be musicians or potential preachers.

A generation ago, youth leaders were almost all male, but in the past decade a number of churches began hiring female youth leaders. As a result, boys are leaving. One church I know hired a female youth leader; within six months 75 percent of the boys had disappeared. I wish this weren't the case. Sounds so sexist—but it's the truth. Teenage boys will not willingly follow a female role model.

As an example of how to do youth group for boys, I would refer you to Young Life Club. This outreach has been targeting unchurched youth since the 1940s. Young Life clubs still do youth group the old-fashioned way—meeting in homes, with a few fun songs, games, skits, and activities. The talk from the youth leader (usually a male) is brief and always focused on Jesus. The whole meeting is done in less than an hour. The fun elements keep boys engaged long enough to be caught in the orbit of men who care for them. Through that relationship, God does his work.

There's even a movement to bring young male initiation back into the church. A number of congregations have adopted a program called "Raising a Modern-Day Knight," the brainchild of Men's Fraternity founder Robert Lewis. The men of the church create manhood "ordeals" for their sons. The ordeals can be quite elaborate and difficult. Once the young men complete their ordeals, the men of the church gather for a knighthood ceremony, to welcome the knights into the community of men.[4]

In an earlier chapter, I excoriated Sunday school publishers for turning Jesus into a smiling Jewish camp counselor. Well, the publishers of youth Bibles are getting things right. Kids' Bibles used to feature cover paintings of Jesus and the children. But today's youth Bibles show a variety of images, some of which are quite adventurous.

There are Bibles covered in camouflage, aluminum, and tattered denim. There's even a *Boys Bible* targeted at eight-to-twelve-year-olds, which promises to help boys find "gross and gory Bible stuff."[5] I'm thinking about ordering one myself.

One other development on the Scripture front—there are New Testaments that look like magazines. They're called BibleZines. There are separate versions for teen girls and teen guys.[6] The girl version looks like a glamour magazine, while the guy version features a skateboarder on the cover. Brilliant—boys can read Scripture at school without looking like a Holy Joe.

o o o

Chuck Stecker once spoke to a woman who serves as a ministry leader in her local church, and he described her attitude: "With complete candor, she said that she would be willing to cancel every program in the church that did not relate directly to developing men into leaders. 'In the long run,' she said, 'every other phase of ministry would be much stronger if the men in the church would develop into the leaders that God has called them to be.'"[7]

Here's a mind bender: What if we canceled the children's ministry and put that effort into building up the men of the church? I firmly believe that such an approach would, in the long run, win more youth to Christ. It would also save more marriages and produce happier women. Children's ministry and youth ministry are good things— but spiritually healthy male role models are the best thing.

Chapter 22

MEN, PRAYER, AND A
FEW OTHER THINGS

IN THE CHURCHES OF MY YOUTH, THE PASTOR WOULD FREQUENTLY call on a layperson to close the worship service in prayer. If he wanted a long, articulate prayer, he would call on a woman. But if he wanted a short prayer, he'd call on a man. Men's closing prayers often sounded like this: "Dear Lord, thank you for this day. Thank you for this opportunity to gather together to worship you. Watch over us and protect us as we go, and bring us back safely next week. In Jesus' name we pray. Amen."

Women's prayers not only were longer but often included a sentence or two that proved they had been listening. "Heavenly Father, as Pastor Matt reminded us, please help us to be better witnesses to our friends and neighbors." But men's closing prayers were always generic—as if the poor guy had already forgotten the entire sermon.

So what's up with men and prayer? Why are they so lousy at praying aloud? Why don't they ask for prayer? Why do so few pray with their wives?

Once again, you can blame the church system. Christians have created a set of expectations that make it harder on men to pray in public.

MEN AND PRAYER-SPEAK

Christians speak conversationally to one another, but not to God. When addressing the Almighty, they lapse into a strange language I call *prayer-speak*.

There are several different dialects of prayer-speak. The most common dialect of my childhood was King James Prayer-Speak. It sounds like this: "We beseech thee, O Lord, that thou wouldst shew thyself amongst us this day." We address God as if he were still living in the age of Shakespeare.

Another popular dialect is High Church Prayer-Speak. The pastor comes slowly to the pulpit and begins his supplication, "Let us pray. [*Pause*] Heavenly Father [*pause*], we come now [*pause*] as your humble [*pause*] servants." Each . . . word . . . is enunciated . . . slowly . . . and . . . distinctly. High Church Prayer-Speak sounds very dignified—and very staged.

When I was a teenager, a friend invited me to a Pentecostal church, where I discovered a third dialect: Holy Ghost Prayer-Speak. The minister prayed in a loud, aggressive voice, "Father, we pray that yo' *powah* would fall! Halle-*lujah*, Father. We invoke the holy name of *Jeeee*-zus!" The louder and more vigorously he prayed, the more amens he got from the assembly.

But it was during a youth Bible study that I discovered the lingua franca of small group intercession: Generic Evangelical Prayer-Speak. Read this passage aloud as quickly as you can, and see if it doesn't sound familiar:

> Father God, we just thank you for this day, blessed Father, and Father God, we just ask you to be with us, Father God, and we just want to praise your holy name for the many blessings you bestow upon us, Father God, and Father God, we just ask you to touch us, Father, touch us deeply, and Father God, we just come to you now, bringing our petitions before the throne of grace, dear God, and Father . . .

Generic Evangelical Prayer-Speak is a nonstop speech to God, with frequent repetitions of his blessed, holy name, punctuated by the word *just*. The most proficient prayer-speakers add an occasional tongue-click to emphasize their sincerity, like this: "Let's pray. [*Tongue-click*] God, we just love you. And God [*tongue-click*], we just thank you for the many blessings you give us . . ."

Now, I realize that prayer-speakers are sincere Christians who want to communicate with God. I'm not accusing anyone of hypocrisy or deception. But prayer-speak is having an unintended side effect: it's literally intimidating men into silence.

Sam sits in church (or small group), listening to longtime Christians communicating with God in prayer-speak. He thinks, *I'd like to pray, but I can't pray like that*. It's hard enough for Sam to have a conversation with someone who doesn't talk back (audibly). Requiring him to do so in a foreign dialect raises the bar too high.

You may be thinking, *Sam doesn't have to use prayer-speak. He can talk to God however he wants*. You know this. I know this. But Sam doesn't know this. He wants to fit in, and if the rest of the church uses prayer-speak, he sounds like a dork when he can't. Rather than be embarrassed, he keeps his trap shut. Or he prays short, safe prayers ("Thank you, Lord, for this beautiful day").

As I conclude a seminar, I sometimes ask for a volunteer to pray—without using prayer-speak. Most people can't do it. They usually repeat God's name at least three times, and the word *just* slips in once or twice.

If you want men to pray aloud, make prayer sound like genuine communication. When you pray in a group, speak to Jesus as if he's a real person who actually exists, one who understands modern English. Don't repeat his name over and over. Cut the excess verbiage and vain repetitions of Christianese.[1]

When a man hears Christians talking in everyday language to a real God, he will be encouraged to join in. I long for the day Christians pray like they talk. "Hey God, there's a problem I gotta talk to you about. I am having some car problems, and I don't have the money to fix it. I could really use some help, or I'm going to be hitchhiking." If guys could pray like that, you'd hear more of them praying aloud.

GROUP PRAYER CAN BE TOUGH ON GUYS

Have you sat in a circle of believers for prayer? The leader often begins by saying, "Just pray as you feel led. And I'll close." There's a brief silence. Then a highly verbal woman opens the floodgates of her heart, gushing a torrent of prayer-speak toward the heavenly throne. Five or ten minutes elapse with hardly a breath, comma, or period. Then, silence. Everyone wonders, *Is it my turn?* Eventually someone else starts a prayer-speech. *Okay, guess it wasn't my turn.* We wait for the next opening, but someone jumps right in—*Oh, shoot! It's Annabelle. She's long-winded. Now I forgot what I was going to pray for.* And so on, around the circle.

This format is tough on men for two reasons. First, men are not that good at formulating long speeches to God. Men can usually think of just one or two things to pray about at a time (blame that visual-spatial brain again), so their prayers sound short and stubby compared to the women's. Second, the pauses make men nervous. Guys would prefer to know it's their turn. They are reluctant to jump in because they don't want to start the same moment someone else does (this is called a *prayer wreck*).

To help men pray, I recommend that small groups adopt one of these strategies (but not both) at prayer time:

1. Pass an object around the circle, such as a tennis ball. Any object will do. When you have the object, you can pray aloud, or you can pass it to the next person. Everyone knows when it's his or her turn to pray. And men have time to think about what they're going to say.
2. Teach the group to pray "popcorn prayers." These are short, single-topic prayers that people offer up as the Spirit leads. People can pray as often as they want, as long as they keep it short. Popcorn prayers sound like this:

ED. God, I still need a job. Help me find one.

CARISSA. Lord, my mom has been sick for a week. I ask
you to heal her.

ED. And please heal my neighbor Joel, who's battling
throat cancer.

WANDA. God, one of my kids has a bully in his class, and
we don't know what to do. He doesn't want to go to
school. Please help us.

After a while the corn stops popping; the leader asks, "Any more
prayers? [*Pause*] Okay, Lord, thank you for hearing our prayers. Amen."

Once guys get used to one of these two formats, they usually
pray more. Passing an object eliminates prayer wrecks and the pregnant pauses. Popcorn prayers relieve men of the pressure to "get it all
in" during their turn. With popcorn prayers there's still the possibility of a prayer wreck, but it's no big deal because you're not trying to
hold a bunch of requests in your head. Next time you're praying in a
group with men, give one of these ideas a try.

PRAYER MUSHROOMS FREAK MEN OUT

Have you heard of a *prayer mushroom*? You know what I'm talking
about: Brother Alex asks for prayer, and soon a crowd has gathered
around him, placing their hands all over his body. With every head
bowed and every eye closed, Alex must sit still as a rock while prayers
go on for five, ten, fifteen minutes, or longer. After many a pregnant
pause, someone finally has the courage to utter a forceful, "amen," but
then Brother Alex may have to stand up and hug a bunch of strangers.

Why do guys fear the mushroom? Men's ministry expert Dan
Schaeffer reminds us that women equate closeness with safety. Men
equate personal space with safety.[2] Prayer mushrooms violate personal space. A man's instinct is to flee. His testosterone makes it hard
to sit still. And having strange hands all over his body is worse than
having a squirrel loose in his jockeys.

I feel no pity for Brother Alex. He asked for it. No, I'm worried about the other guys in the room. They see what just happened to Alex, and they're terrified that it might happen to them. So they keep their prayer requests to themselves, because they don't want to end up under the mushroom. Pretty soon you've got twelve women and one old man coming forward for prayer.

Some men's groups are experimenting with an alternative to the prayer mushroom. It's called a *prayer force*. Brother Alex sits or stands in the middle of a semicircle. The men step forward and pray for him one at a time. Some may lay hands on Alex. Others may just pray from where they stand. This format is less intimidating to guys and can be tremendously powerful in men's lives. (For a video demonstration of a prayer force at work, visit my website, www .churchformen.com.)

WHY MEN DON'T PRAY WITH THEIR WIVES

Early in our marriage my wife and I tried praying together. She usually went first, and her prayers were long and eloquent, delivered in the fluent prayer-speak she learned as a preacher's daughter. Then it was my turn. I felt a subtle pressure to match her lengthy epistle. I couldn't do it, so I gave up.

Women, if you are praying with a man, please start in silence. Give him the first word. Then as you take your turn, match his length and cadence. If he offers a halting eight-word prayer, you do the same.

If the man you're married to still won't pray with you, there's one more thing you can try. According to one study, married couples who pray together are 90 percent more likely to report higher satisfaction with their sex life than couples who do not pray together. Also, women who pray with their partner tend to be more orgasmic.[3] If the promise of coital bliss doesn't drive your husband to his knees, nothing will.

ASSUMPTION: THE BEST PRAYER IS LONG PRAYER

In my thirty-plus years of attending church, I've heard many a story about some great man of prayer who rose daily at 3 a.m. and prayed four to five hours before beginning his day. These anecdotes were supposed to inspire, but they always left me feeling inadequate—like I was shortchanging God if I only had, say, fifteen minutes to give him.

Then I read what Jesus said about prayer. He warned us not to keep babbling on, like the pagans, "for they think they will be heard because of their many words."[4] He followed with a model prayer of exactly sixty-six words.[5] It can be prayed in fewer than thirty seconds.

Nothing in Scripture suggests that long prayers are better than short ones. The Bible recommends consistency and frequency, not length.

SPIRITUAL DISCIPLINES AND MEN

What are the "Big Four" spiritual disciplines you hear about in church today? *Read your Bible. Pray. Give. Go to church.* So say Protestant ministers the world over. Women outperform men in all these disciplines.

Of course, the Big Four disciplines are helpful and necessary for spiritual growth—but they have a dark side. They tend to isolate men. *Read your Bible* (alone). *Pray* (alone). *Give* (in secret). *Go to church* (alone in a crowd). Week after week, we implore men to practice their faith alone—and so they do. After a while, men perceive their faith as a God-and-me thing. Once a man thinks this way, he's vulnerable to sin and self-righteousness. A fellow who practices his faith alone is like a baseball pitcher without any fielders behind him. He is under enormous pressure to be perfect. If he makes the slightest mistake, his opponent will score easily.

I'm going to step out on a limb. I believe the most important valuable spiritual discipline for today's men is the discipline of *friendship.* This is not to diminish the importance of the Big Four. But the men who stay faithful to God are those who walk closely with other Christian men—not necessarily those who read the Scriptures day and night. (If this were the case, Jesus would have chosen Pharisees for his apostles.) I've devoted chapter 24 to this important topic.

PRACTICE SAFE HUGGING

In chapter 12, we talked about the church's "hugging addiction." In some churches the pastor invites everyone to hug everyone else. It seems like these congregations always have at least one big, sweaty guy who corners men, wraps them in a bear hug, and "shares the love of Jeeee-zus."

So is it ever appropriate for men to hug in church? Of course. When greeting a close friend, a hug is appropriate. If a friend is upset and seems to want an embrace, go ahead and offer one. If a man in your small group is going through a divorce, and he's dissolved in tears, then a hug is the best gift you can give him.

But what about hugs during the worship service? That's a little trickier. Here's my advice:

1. Don't suggest that people hug. If people want to lock up, that's their business.
2. Don't hug people you're not close to. Male or female. It's creepy.
3. Practice "safe hugging." There are two acceptable forms of man hug: the one-arm reach, and the handshake-and-hug combo. These hugs are better for men because there's no possibility of crotch contact.

Man hugs should be brief and accompanied by a pat on the back, preferably one that stings a little bit. Man hugs should feel brotherly, not romantic. I demonstrate safe hugging on my website, www.churchformen.com.

o o o

At the end of every episode of the *Red Green Show*, the men of Possum Lodge stand and recite the Man Prayer:

I'm a man,
and I can change,
if I have to,
I guess.

The Man Prayer sums up in thirteen little words how men feel about themselves. They know they need to change—and God has something to do with it—but they aren't all that excited about it.

Men change when they minister to others—and when they allow others to minister to them. Ministry for and to men is the topic of our next two chapters.

Chapter 23

HOW MEN MINISTER
TO OTHERS

ALL EYES WERE ON PASTOR KEITH, WHO HAD BEEN PROMISING FOR
weeks to make an important announcement. "As of next month," the
pastor said, "we are canceling the nursery and Sunday school. We will
no longer offer weddings, baptisms, baby showers, or funerals. We are
dropping our choir and pulling out of our partnership with the soup
kitchen. Instead, we're going to minister in a new way. Our children's
ministry will be based on sports leagues. We will offer free automo-
tive repairs to the working poor. We will provide carpentry, plumbing,
and electrical upgrades to seniors' homes. We will deploy our members
as security ambassadors, walking the streets of high-crime neighbor-
hoods. And our missions team will dig water wells in Honduras."

Women, how would you feel if your pastor made such an
announcement? How well does this roster of ministries match your
skills and gifts?

Now you know how men feel. Generally speaking, men's gifts
and abilities do not match the ministry needs of the typical American
congregation of about one hundred people. Men are square pegs,
trying to fit into a sea of round holes.

You may be thinking, *What do you mean, round holes? Men are
welcome in every volunteer position.* It's a question not of welcome but
of expertise. As we saw in chapter 11, most jobs in the church require

verbal and relational skills that men may not possess. They demand proficiency with children, music, teaching, hospitality, or cooking, areas where women typically have more experience. A woman is so much more valuable in church than a man because her natural gifts and life experiences enable her to fill so many slots.

Dr. John Gray warns, "Not to be needed is slow death for a man."[1] You crush a man's spirit when you reject his gifts. So how can we make men feel needed again?

GIVE MEN OPPORTUNITIES TO USE THEIR SKILLS AND GIFTS

Central Baptist Church in Livingston, Texas, sponsors a men's chain-saw team. Each man buys and maintains his own saw. Whenever a hurricane, tornado, or ice storm strikes, the men rush to the scene to cut fallen timber until power is restored and homes can be reoccupied.

Herb Reese of New Commandment Men's Ministries takes a group of four men and places a widow or single mother under their care. Once a month the men do handyman projects around her house, work on her car, help her balance her checkbook, whatever she needs. Herb says, "One guy told me, 'I like this. I don't feel like a wimp or a wuss.'" Herb continues, "For a lot of men, this is the first time they really understand the love of Christ. It's practical love. It's something guys can talk about on Monday morning with their coworkers."

Ministries like these change the core competencies of a Christian. The star disciple is no longer the best singer, teacher, or caregiver. A man who can wield a saw feels valued and needed. He's got a skill he can use for God's kingdom—something he can do better than his wife. It's his turn to shine.

GIVE MEN A PATH TO WALK OR A LADDER TO CLIMB

Men must sense they are on a path that's leading them toward some-thing, or they will run aground. The path must be explained and presented in visual form so men can chart their progress. For example, Saddleback uses a baseball diamond; your goal is home plate. Church of the Resurrection in Kansas uses a mountain diagram; your goal is the summit. Your men must know they are pressing toward a target, gaining skill and responsibility as their level of commitment increases.

GIVE MEN EXTERNAL FOCUS

Evangelist Luis Palau says, "The church is like manure. Pile it up and it stinks up the neighborhood; spread it out and it enriches the world." Eric Swanson studies healthy churches, and without exception they are externally focused: their goal is to make a significant and sustainable difference in the lives of people around them.[2]

Fellowship Bible Church in Little Rock models external focus through its small group system. New members are placed in small groups for instruction and nurture. But after three years, they're kicked out into a common cause group that serves the community. Founding pastor Robert Lewis points out, "That's where men flourish, because men are action oriented."[3]

So-called liberation churches demonstrate a specialized form of external focus. A number of urban churches have discovered they can attract men through social activism. These churches are committed to turning their economically depressed communities around through drug-treatment programs, job-training centers, and economic-development projects. Many men are reached through these churches because they see the difference they make in the community.

GIVE MEN BIG PROJECTS THAT
CAPTURE THEIR IMAGINATIONS

Corporate America has learned the importance of BHAGs to motivate men. BHAG stands for Big, Hairy, Audacious Goal. Adam Hamilton built America's fastest-growing Methodist church by dreaming

God-sized dreams. He notes, "Too many churches dream safe, easily attainable dreams. They don't risk, they don't require faith, they don't need God in order to be accomplished."[4] Bruce Wilkinson says God's people "are expected to attempt something large enough that failure is guaranteed . . . unless God steps in."[5]

GIVE MEN ADVENTURE

Randy was a nominal churchgoer for many years, but he never really came alive in his faith until he took a two-week mission trip to Peru to build a water project in an impoverished village. "I had no idea how real the gospel was until I went on this trip. We depended on God every minute of every day," he says. "He helped us through one tight spot after another. As we were taking off, our airplane was hit by bullets from a rebel paramilitary group. It was like being in the book of Acts."

Randy returned from Peru a changed man. Once he realized how powerful and real God is, he began a daily walk with him. He stepped up to leadership in church. He and his wife began praying together for the first time. Randy continued to support missions in South America, and he returned the next year with a bigger team. He shared his story with his American neighbors, and they started coming to church. Adventures with Christ change men in a way simple church attendance never could.

DEPLOY MEN IN SERVANT EVANGELISM

Traditional approaches to evangelism leave many men cold. Most men don't want to go door-to-door selling Jesus. Talk about an exercise in futility. But Vineyard Community Church in Cincinnati found that men will gladly witness by serving the community. They fix up houses, pass out drinks, clean bathrooms, and wrap packages. They accept no donations and often utter only one sentence: "We just want to show you God's love in a practical way." This kind of evangelism gives the church a positive image in the community and motivates people to visit.

DON'T KEEP WHAT YOUR CHURCH IS DOING A SECRET

Churches that reach men celebrate loudly and publicly what God is doing in their midst. They seek publicity. They advertise. This would seem to contradict Christ's command that we do good works in secret. I think this command applies to individuals, not churches. People shouldn't draw attention to their personal piety, but when God is moving powerfully in a church, get the word out.

CHARGE MEN MONEY

If you want a man to show up for a class, retreat, or seminar, charge him something. Promise Keepers learned this lesson the hard way in 1998. The decision was made to stop charging admission to PK stadium rallies in the hope that more lower-income men would attend. Instead, attendance plummeted. Why? If a man has to lay his money down, he'll be there. But if a man pays nothing, he's more likely to back out at the last minute.

You don't have to charge a lot. My church charges a ten-dollar registration fee for each class. This modest materials fee is enough to get men to commit, but not enough to discourage low-income folks from signing up. (We always make scholarships available for the truly needy.) This practice is a far cry from setting up money changers in the temple. The goal is not to enrich the church, but to ensure a higher level of commitment from men.

OFFER PERSONAL INVITATIONS TO CHURCH

Don't overlook the obvious. Nothing brings a man to church or to a ministry event like a personal invitation from a man he respects. One study found 63 percent of unchurched Americans would likely visit a church if invited by a friend or relative.[6] According to Man in the Mirror Ministries, you can triple your attendance at men's events by forming a call team responsible for phoning and inviting ten men each.[7]

RECOGNIZE THE IMPORTANCE OF ENTRY AND EXIT POINTS

Once a man begins attending your church, it's often helpful to have entry-level ministry opportunities. Parking and ushering are two of the most popular ways to introduce men to ministry. But don't leave a man in an entry-level job for ten years; give him a next step to move into as he matures in faith and service.

Also, don't forget exit points. Rick Warren writes, "To resign from a ministry in some churches, you've either got to die, leave the church or be willing to live with intense guilt."[8] One of the main reasons men do not step up to minister is the never-ending commitment that's implied. But ask a man for a short-term commitment, and he's more likely to say yes. When he reaches the finish line, celebrate.

MOST IMPORTANT: AS MEN MINISTER, MAKE SURE THEY'RE ALSO BEING DISCIPLED

This is a major tragedy of today's church: we put men to work for God, but we do not disciple them. Pat Morley tells a poignant story from his childhood:

> My dear father and mother, who both passed away last year, joined a church for the religious and moral instruction of their four young boys. Our church had a vision for putting my Dad to work—he became the top layman by age 40. But our church had no vision for helping him become a disciple—a Godly man, husband, and father.
>
> As a result, when my Dad was 40 and I was in the 10th grade and my youngest brother was in the 3rd grade, my parents burned out. Our family left the church. My parents never returned. It put our family into a downward spiral from which we have still not fully recovered.[9]

o o o

Christ left us with a simple assignment: make disciples. But our current model—pumping men full of Bible knowledge and setting them to work in the church—is not getting the job done. In the next chapter we identify the missing element that's keeping men from becoming fully devoted followers of Christ.

Chapter 24

HOW TO MINISTER TO MEN

IN 2008, I HAD THE PLEASURE OF SITTING DOWN TO INTERVIEW A man who has done the impossible. His name is Mark Driscoll. He's built a huge church in the capital of American secularism: Seattle, Washington. Even more remarkable, Mars Hill Church is brimming with men. Many of them are young, single men, the hardest demographic group to reach. (You can watch the interview on my website, www.churchformen.com.)

I asked Mark, "Does Mars Hill Church have a men's ministry program?" He smiled, and with a chuckle said, "Mars Hill Church *is* a men's ministry program."[1]

o o o

Your church does not need a men's ministry program to reach men. In fact, I would not recommend you start one.

I'm not anti–men's ministry. Many churches have thriving programs for their men. They're doing terrific, transformational work.

But if your church does not have a men's program, there's no need to add one—not yet. Here are the facts about men's ministry programs:

- Fewer than 10 percent of US congregations offer one.
- Starting a men's ministry program is a ton of work.

- Only about 20 percent of your male church attendees will ever participate.
- Young men almost never participate.
- About 90 percent of men's ministry programs fail within two years of launch.

So if you build it, will they come? Not likely. Most guys could not care less about men's ministry. They're busy. They're working. They're pursuing their passions. Or they're doing exactly what we always tell them to do: being good husbands and fathers. Going to their kids' activities. Spending time with their wives. When do they have time for men's ministry?

Driscoll adds, "You're going to get one shot at the men, and that's on Sunday morning. So you have to reach them with what you're already doing." Starting a men's ministry program will benefit, at most, 20 percent of your men. But making your existing ministries man-friendly will benefit 100 percent of your men.

Okay. So you're thinking about turning your church into a men's ministry program. Where do you begin?

1. Examine everything your church does through the eyes of a man, and ask yourself, "Would this intrigue/encourage/interest a guy?"
2. Then start making little changes. One song at a time. One sermon at a time. One lace doily at a time.
3. Not to be self-serving, but study this book with your staff and elders. Make sure everyone is working off the same page.

That's how a church becomes a men's ministry. It's not about turning the worship service into a monster truck rally. It's about taking what's already being done and removing the man-repellent stuff. Many of these changes occur in the background. They're imperceptible to the majority of parishioners.

Once your Sunday routine becomes a haven for men, you'll see more of them in church. So what do you do with 'em? How do you help them become genuine followers of Jesus?

At this point it may be time to start thinking about offering some ministry programs for men. Before you do, read the story of Tony.

Tony went to a men's Bible study at his church—once. First, the men sat in a circle and sang praise songs for about ten minutes. Tony was asked to introduce himself and share about his life. Next, he was paired with a stranger and asked to share one of his deepest fears. Then, everyone was asked to share a prayer need or a praise report. The men read from the Bible, taking turns around the circle. Finally, the men stood in a circle and held hands for what seemed like hours, while one by one they bared their souls to God. The guy next to Tony prayed for seven minutes straight, and his palms were sweaty. Once the meeting was over, Tony didn't stay for cookies. He hasn't been back.

Men's ministry so often falters for this simple reason: it's actually women's ministry for men. When Christian men gather, they're expected to build relationships the way women do. Men's ministry is built around the needs and expectations of women—or more precisely, the churchy guys who show up for men's ministry events. So the men's retreat features singing, hugging, and handholding. Men sit in circles and listen, read, or share. We keep our conversations clean, polite, and nonconfrontational.

While there's nothing wrong with men doing these things, it feels feminine to a lot of guys. So they stay home.

The two predominant models of men's ministry today are the small group Bible study, and the large group fellowship/teaching event. Large group events include the weekly crack-of-dawn men's teaching session, the Saturday morning men's pancake breakfast, and the annual men's retreat.

Both small group Bible studies and large group teaching events are very good at getting men into the Bible. They help men apply scriptural truths to their daily lives in a masculine context. But few men are partaking. In many cases the problem isn't the content—it's the format. Bible studies and teaching sessions are both academic exercises. They tend to reward the same men who do well in church: the verbal and studious. And they do a lousy job helping men make friends—which is what men are really looking for today.

o o o

My mother used to tell me, "David, take a good look at your friends, because that's who you're becoming like." If you want men to become like Jesus, put them in regular contact with peers who are following Jesus. Boys who run with a pack of Christian friends stay truer to Christ's teachings. Men who regularly walk with Christian brothers grow deep in faith, strong in service, and extravagant in love. Men who have male buddies in the church rally behind its ministry, pastor, and mission. It's truly amazing the difference a close friend or two can make.

But men have a hard time finding friends—even in church. A study by the Gallup organization found that just 35 percent of men had a best friend in their congregation.[2] A study of highly committed Methodist men (86 percent were every-Sunday churchgoers) found that just 28 percent had a close male friend who knows or supports him.[3]

Here are four basic truths about men and relationships:

1. Relationships scare a man to death, but they are his deepest need.
2. Men don't usually use the word *relationship* about other men.
3. Women bond face-to-face, whereas men bond side by side.
4. Enduring male bonds are formed under pressure.

Let's examine these one at a time.

1. RELATIONSHIPS SCARE A MAN TO DEATH, BUT THEY ARE HIS DEEPEST NEED. Many men don't see relationships as the answer; they see them as the problem. Relationships complicate their otherwise straightforward lives. Men who are competent at work and on the golf course may not be

so hot at relationships. As a result, most men don't bother to pursue these vital relationships, because they seem to be more trouble than they're worth.

2. **MEN DON'T USUALLY USE THE WORD** *RELATIONSHIP* **ABOUT OTHER MEN.** In men's minds, the term *relationship* usually refers to a male-female couple. Men don't have *relationships*. Instead, they do things together. As we saw in chapter 12, Ron would never say to his friend, "Bruce, can we have a personal relationship?" This would violate the man laws because it was not expressed in terms of activity. The man-accepted approach would be for Ron to say, "Bruce, let's go shoot some baskets after work tonight."

3. **WOMEN BOND FACE-TO-FACE, WHEREAS MEN BOND SIDE BY SIDE.** Masculine friendships form while guys are doing something else. Like trying to beat each other to the hoop. Or fishing. Or working on cars. Have you ever noticed that when a man wants to talk, he'll often suggest going for a drive? He wants to communicate the masculine way, which is shoulder to shoulder.

4. **ENDURING MALE BONDS ARE FORMED UNDER PRESSURE.** When men struggle together, they bond. Soldiers who survive a battle are often friends for life. Same goes for athletic teammates who fight together to win a title. Fraternity brothers bond not at the party but by surviving the hangover together. Men who live through a harrowing experience often emerge as brothers. The deeper the struggle, the stronger the bond.

o   o   o

When the Lord started his ministry, one of his first tasks was to gather twelve men and forge them into a band of brothers. Did it ever occur to you that Jesus might have been trying to show us something? Maybe the basic unit of God's church is not the individual, the committee, the Bible study circle, or even the congregation. Maybe it's the small men's group. What if the key to transforming our world is transforming men in little teams?

Think of the sheer lunacy of Jesus' method. The Lord bypassed the top draft picks, choosing instead a dozen run-of-the-mill guys. They had jobs. Some had wives. Several were foul-mouthed commercial fishermen. One was a politico. One had a problem with greed. One was a government employee. There was not a religious expert among them. Indeed, if you picked twelve guys at random from the back rows of your church, you'd probably assemble a more talented, educated group than Jesus did.

Now, what was Christ trying to tell us by this? *Structure matters.* You can gather a handful of common men, and if you weld them into a team—a true team—you can change the world with them. How you organize and deploy your men is just as important as what you teach them, and it's more important than how talented they are.

Larry Brown knows this. He was coach of the US men's basketball team at the 2004 Summer Olympics in Athens. Talk about a favorite: the Americans entered the tournament with an all-time Olympic record of 109 wins and 2 losses. They had taken the gold medal twelve times in fourteen attempts. Brown's team was stacked with National Basketball Association all-stars. But Team USA lost three of its five games and struggled to finish with the bronze.

How could the most talented players on the planet lose to teams from Puerto Rico, Lithuania, and Argentina? A sportswriter for the Associated Press put it this way: "A hastily assembled assortment of NBA stars couldn't beat a better team."

In the church, we make the same mistake as Team USA. We hastily assemble groups to study the Bible, pray, serve in the community, make music, and so on. But we fail to forge these groups into genuine teams. And men suffer for it.

How was Jesus able to take a dozen scrubs and turn them into stars? He called a finite number of men into his inner circle. He took personal responsibility for their growth. He became thoroughly involved in their lives for an extended period of time. He made their development his top priority. He saw these men as his earthly legacy. Then, once they were ready, he sent them out to do as he did.

In other words, Jesus served as a *spiritual father* to the Twelve.

Spiritual father? You may never have heard the term. It comes from Paul's first letter to the Corinthians: "I do not write these things to shame you, but as my beloved children I warn you. For though you might have ten thousand instructors in Christ, yet you do not have many fathers; for in Christ Jesus I have begotten you through the gospel."⁴

The situation in Paul's day was not much different from ours. Modern churches have ten thousand men who want to preach and teach. But how many fathers do we have? How many men are willing to put their time and treasure at risk in order to personally grow other men to maturity?

Think about your church. Is there even one man who is raising up disciples the way Jesus did?

- He takes a finite number of men into his inner circle.
- He takes personal responsibility for their spiritual growth.
- He becomes thoroughly involved in their lives for an extended time.
- He makes their development his top priority.
- He sees them as his earthly legacy.
- Once they are ready, he sends them out to do as he did.

I would guess that in most churches not one man is doing this kind of work with other men. Pastors certainly don't have time do it, with all the demands we heap upon them.

A man cannot rebuild his life alone. He not only needs God, but he must also have the security and support of a small group of guys he knows and trusts. Once he is restored to spiritual health, he's already surrounded by brothers who will help him grow in faith and help him if he falls. This is how the church is meant to function.

o   o   o

Eighty percent of the citizens of Milwaukee, Wisconsin, will tell you they're either Catholic or Lutheran, but only 21 percent go to church. It's one of the most religious but least churched cities in America.

In the early 1990s, Elmbrook Church in suburban Milwaukee hired Steve Sonderman as the men's minister. In his first month on the job, Steve held a funeral for the men's pancake breakfast. Instead of trying to gather a big crowd of guys to listen to a speaker, Steve started discipling a handful of men. Not superstars, just regular knuckleheads. He taught them from the Bible. He took them into the community. Steve was tough on them. He set very high expectations. Being discipled by Steve Sonderman was like hugging a cactus. It was part seminary, part missionary, part coronary.

When he felt his men were ready, Steve sent them to disciple other men. He followed their progress and helped them as challenges cropped up.

Today, Elmbrook Church has some fifteen hundred men meeting in small groups all over southeastern Wisconsin. Each is led by a competently trained spiritual father (though Steve doesn't use that term). The curriculum Steve wrote, under the manly moniker *Top Gun*, is being used to disciple men the world over.[5]

Elmbrook has accomplished this without a weekly men's meeting. No auditorium filled with men listening to a teacher. No annual men's retreat. Not even matching polo shirts. Instead, the entire men's ministry consists of little bands of brothers living the Christian life in teams. As the groups proliferate, men with leadership potential are trained and sent to form new groups. The ministry grows one spiritual father at a time.

Here's the best part: a new believer can have a spiritual father and a band of brothers around him within minutes of his decision. In most churches we pray with converts, pat them on the back, and wish them well. During the next eight weeks, more than half of those new believers will disappear, never to be seen in church again. But at Elmbrook, no man gets left behind.

Elmbrook Church has benefited greatly from the presence of so many committed men. The church has enjoyed a long season of growth and peace. It's now the largest church in the state of Wisconsin, welcoming more than eight thousand worshippers on a typical weekend.

Fifteen years ago, Steve Sonderman stood at a crossroads. He could have followed the usual men's ministry script: put on events, try to gather a crowd, try to funnel men into small groups. These large gatherings would have done some good. Men would have been taught God's Word. A few lives might have been nudged in the right direction.

But instead, Steve followed Christ's structural blueprint. He has birthed an army of committed men, organized in little platoons. Men who are being continually strengthened in faith, loving their families, and serving the community. Because of the masculine leadership structure, men finally feel free to sit in circles and share from the heart. Men study the Bible and read Christian books. And guess what? *They like it.*

o   o   o

If you decide to create a ministry program for men, the first question is not, "What am I going to teach?" It should be, "How am I going to organize?" Build a few spiritual fathers, and then put them in charge of a band of brothers. The leader-and-group dynamic is what changes men's lives. Changed men change the world.

There's a great deal of innovation going on in the area of ministry to men. Outdoor ministries are growing. Video curricula are proliferating. And good old-fashioned Bible and book studies are ubiquitous. Men are being transformed on mission trips, by volunteering in their communities, and by serving others. Christian men are learning to have fun together.

Hardly a week goes by that I don't hear about some exciting initiative to reach men and boys—or a church that's growing by building on men. I keep a list of the best on my website, www .churchformen.com.

And I'm working on a men's discipleship regimen that puts bands of brothers with spiritual fathers. The lessons are completely non-academic—even a man who can't read his own name can be discipled with this evolving model. To learn more, visit www.mensleague.org.

Chapter 25

A CHURCH FOR EVERYONE

So who's to blame for Christianity's gender gap? Men? Women? Pastors? Musicians? Authors? Businessmen?

Yes.

We're all part of a religious delivery system that reaches more women than men. Most Christians are happy with this system. It works for us. We've gotten used to Christianity being the way it is, and frankly, we can't imagine it any other way.

Jesus encountered a religious delivery system that worked well for insiders—everyone else be cursed. And it angered him. He said to the Pharisees, "You shut the kingdom of heaven in men's faces. You yourselves do not enter, nor will you let those enter who are trying to."[1]

As I noted in the introduction, the gender gap is widening—but signs of hope abound. Innovative churches and ministries are figuring out how to open the door to men. Here are some bright spots:

Children's Ministry

I'm very excited about what's happening to Sunday school. The big rooms, kinetic lessons, and video curricula are all great for young men. Churches are putting boys with male teachers. Even vacation Bible school curriculum is not as cutesy as it used to be. I just saw one called *Rev It Up: Full Throttle for God*, built on a speedway-racing theme. Every boy in the neighborhood will want to attend that VBS.

Youth Ministry

This is a huge area of concern, as more youth groups move to a praise band model. But on the positive side, many churches are creating very cool spaces for their youth to gather. Large, open rooms with foosball and air hockey tables, along with state-of-the-art video gaming consoles, are becoming more common—giving boys a place and an excuse to hang out with Christian men.

Athletic Ministry

Have you noticed the many college and professional athletes giving glory to God? The tireless work of groups like Athletes in Action and the Fellowship of Christian Athletes is paying huge dividends. And it's providing healthy athletic role models for boys.

Music

There seem to be fewer "Jesus is my boyfriend" songs being sung in church these days. Maybe it's just the churches I frequent, but we may have turned a corner on this one. Songwriters seem to be backing off from the extremely erotic imagery that was so popular in the 2000s. Even Matt Redman, composer of the song "Let my words be few/Jesus I am so in love with you,"[2] has said that he might change that lyric to "I am so in *awe* of you," if he could do it over again.[3] Bully on you, Matt.

And thanks be to God—endless repetition seems to be going out of style. A few years back, worship leaders would repeat-repeat-repeat until they slowly lapsed into a "worship coma." Then, with eyes rolling back in their heads, they would say, "Let's just lift that song of praise to Jesus one more time!" And all the men in the audience would think, *No, let's not!*

o o o

A few weeks ago I was training about eighty ministers in Peoria, Illinois. I started with a question: "Do any of you pastors have more men than women in your church?" Normally when I ask this, no one responds. But to my surprise, one hand shot up in the back row.

The hand had nail polish on it.

The owner of the hand was Rev. Dr. Jennifer Wilson. She's the senior pastor of Grace United Methodist Church in LaSalle, Illinois, a town of about ten thousand people. The church was founded in 1850.

A couple years ago, Jenn was surfing the web, looking for books on church growth. She stumbled across my second book, *How Women Help Men Find God*. She ordered it, read it, and then ordered the original edition of *Why Men Hate Going to Church*.

Her ministry would never be the same. "I started doing all the stuff in your books," she told me. "Other than the Bible, your book has shifted the way I do ministry more than any other book I've read." (I did not pay her to say this.)

The changes at Grace United Methodist were immediate. First, Jenn adjusted her language. "As I write liturgy and prayers and sermons, I'm thinking, *How would a guy like a bricklayer, a farmer, a mechanic, or a line worker hear this?*" She began using more masculine metaphors and illustrations that males could relate to.

Next was the décor. "We opted not to use those hand-sewn banners. No more fabric anything!" Jenn said. Members repainted every wall in guy-friendly tones. There are no more flowers, except the occasional garden-picked arrangement donated by a parishioner. "At Christmas and Easter I asked our people, 'Would you rather buy flowers or feed a family?'" As of this writing, teams of male volunteers are tearing down walls and expanding the A/V area of the church. "We are big into technology," she said.

Then came music. "I looked through the hymnals and I was appalled. The language is overtly feminine. I chucked the music with feminine words or content, which made some of our choir members upset. One quit," she said. "We've brought back the masculine songs— 'A Mighty Fortress,' 'Rise Up O Men of God,' 'Onward Christian Soldiers'—and our older guys are excited and inviting their friends." Grace UMC does not have a praise band. They sing a mix of hymns and praise songs accompanied by organ or piano.

Humor is standard on Sunday morning. So are video clips. "We get the funniest stuff we can off YouTube, and they make great illustrations," she says. "We even changed the background images we put up on the screen. We use guy-friendly natural images, like mountains, stone, and deserts, things like that."

Jenn gathered her team and specifically asked men what they would like to see in the church. The guys mapped out four "Go for the Guys Sundays." The first was called Sports Sunday (wear your favorite team jersey), complete with a huge tailgate party after church. "We had tons of visitors that day. The team—men and women—completely planned and executed the tailgate; I didn't have to do a thing," Jenn said.

Rev. Wilson plans her sermon series with men in mind: "Posers." "GodLoveSex." "Power Play." She often divides her sermon into mini-messages that run about eight to ten minutes. She makes the same point using several different methods. The service is done in an hour.

Since Jennifer Wilson became pastor of Grace UMC, worship attendance has doubled. The church sees new men almost every week. "My confirmation class has seventeen boys and four girls," she says with a laugh. "One of the women in my church is thrilled because her husband is coming to church more now than at any other time in his life. Normally he would be on the golf course on Sunday, but now he rarely misses unless he has to work."

There are still battles to be won at Grace UMC. There's hand holding at the end of the service (though Jenn tells everyone it's optional). Children's education needs a new name (it's still called Sunday school). It's not a perfect church for men, but it's a darn good one.

The median age at Grace UMC is forty-one (the average US Methodist is fifty-seven[4]). There are lots of kids and young couples. Jennifer baptized thirty-seven people last year, and overall attendance is up 8 percent in the past twelve months, to an average of about 275 on Sunday, and 75 Wednesday night. Typically there are more adult men than women in the worship service. And they're not just pew sitters—they're involved. Excited. Volunteering. Bringing their friends. There is even a growing corps of single guys. "I've got two or three men who would die for this church," Jennifer says. "I mean it."

o   o   o

So if a small, rural, liturgical, 160-year-old mainline church that sings hymns accompanied by an organ, led by a woman, can reach men—what's stopping you?

You've tried all the other church-growth strategies. Why not employ the one Jesus used?

Go get some men.

Discussion questions for this chapter are available free at www.churchformen.com/guides.

NOTES

Chapter 1: Perfectly Designed

1. John Gray, *Men Are from Mars, Women Are from Venus* (New York: HarperCollins, 1992), chapter 2.
2. Woody L. Davis, "Evangelizing the Pre-Christian Male," Net Results, June 2001, 4, www.netresults.org.

Chapter 2: Yes, There Really Is a Gender Gap

1. Barna Research Online, "Women Are the Backbone of Christian Congregations in America," 6 March 2000, www.barna.org.
2. Leon J. Podles, *The Church Impotent: The Feminization of Christianity* (Dallas: Spence Publishing, 1999), ix.
3. Barna, "Women Are the Backbone."
4. Reihan Salam, "Equality Thanks to Capitalism," *Forbes*, 8 February 2010. In January 2010, women outnumbered men in the nonfarm labor force for the first time.
5. Barna, "Women Are the Backbone."
6. Rebecca Barnes and Lindy Lowry: "Special Report: The American Church in Crisis," *Outreach*, May/June 2006. Over a third of Americans claim to have gone to church during the prior week, but by studying actual attendance figures, the authors found that true attendance was about half that number.
7. I base this on numerous e-mails I've received from pastors reporting gender gaps as high as 10 to 1. Churches in Asia seem to suffer the highest gaps.

8. "Myths About Worshipers and Congregations: Results from the U.S. Congregational Life Survey," 2002, www.uscongregations.org /myths.htm.

9. ABC News/Beliefnet poll conducted 19–20 February 2002 among a random national sample of 1,008 adults. Posted at www.abcnews .com. The results have a 3-point error margin.

10. I came up with this figure by taking the US Census 2000 numbers for total married adults and overlaying Barna Research's year 2000 percentages of male versus female attendance at weekly worship services. The figures suggest at least 24.5 million married women attend church on a given weekend, but only 19 million married men attend. That's 5.5 million more women, or 22.5 percent. The actual gender gap figure may be even higher, because married people attend church in much greater numbers than singles.

11. "Myths About Worshipers and Congregations."

12. ABC News/Beliefnet poll conducted 19 February 2002.

13. Dr. Mark Chaves, "National Congregations Study of 1998." The study finds 92.2 percent of churches that identify themselves as "Black Christian" draw a crowd that's 56 percent or more female.

14. ABC/Beliefnet poll.

15. Chaves, "National Congregations Study of 1998."

16. Edward Thompson, "Beneath the Status Characteristic: Gender Variations in Religiousness," *Journal for the Scientific Study of Religion*, 1991, 30.

17. Barry A. Kosmin and Seymore P. Lachman, *One Nation Under God: Religion in Contemporary American Society* (New York: Harmony Books, 1993), 220.

18. "American Religious Identification Survey," Graduate Center, City University of New York, 2001, exhibit 11. Results are a combination of the 1990 and 2001 studies.

19. Podles, *The Church Impotent*, 26.

20. Joshua P. Georgen, "Looking for a Few Good Men," LAM News Service (Mexico City), 29 April 2003, www.lam.org.

21. E-mail correspondence with the missionaries, January 2011. Read my blog entry on this phenomenon at http://bit.ly/LACGaps.

22. Barna, "Women Are the Backbone."

23. Albert L. Winseman, "Religion and Gender: A Congregation Divided," 3 December 2002, Gallup Tuesday Briefing, Religion and Values Content Channel, www.gallup.com.

24. Ibid., Part III, 17 December 2002.

25. Ibid.

26. Barna, "Women Are the Backbone of Christian Congregations in America."

27. Ibid.

28. United Methodist Church website, www.umc.org. Figures are for 1999, rounded to the nearest thousand.

29. BSF International website, "Find a Class," http://www .bsfinternational.org.

30. John P. Bartkowski, "Whatever Happened to the Promise Keepers?" Hartford Institute for Religion Research website, www .hirr.hartsem.edu/research/religion_family_pksummary.html.

Chapter 3: Men: Who Needs 'Em?

1. "Why Religion Matters: The Impact of Religious Practice on Social Stability," Heritage Foundation Backgrounder, 25 January 1996, www .heritage.org.

2. Penny Edgell (Becker) and Heather Hofmeister, "Work, Family and Religious Involvement for Men and Women," Hartford Institute for Religion Research, http://hirr.hartsem.edu/research /edgell-gender.html.

3. Christian Smith and Phillip Kim, "Religious Youth Are More Likely to Have Positive Relationships with Their Fathers," University of North Carolina at Chapel Hill, 12 July 2002, findings based on the National Longitudinal Survey of Youth (1997).

4. C. Kirk Hadaway, FACTs on Growth, Faith Communities Today, 2005, http://faithcommunitiestoday.org/sites/all/themes/factzen4/files/ CongGrowth.pdf.

5. George Gallup Jr., "Why Are Women More Religious?" 17 December 2002, Gallup Tuesday Briefing, Religion and Values, www.gallup.com.

6. Anne and Bill Moir, Why Men Don't Iron (New York: Citadel Press, 1999), 131.

7. Raksha Arora, "Female Investors Retain Bearish Outlook," 21 October 2003, Gallup Tuesday Briefing, Finance and Commerce Content Channel, www.gallup.com.

8. See Matthew 25:14–30.

9. Jesus warned those who would abandon the rules, "If you reject even the least important command in the Law and teach others to do the same, you will be the least important person in the kingdom of heaven" (Matt. 5:19 CEV).

10. National Council of Churches of Christ, "Yearbook of American and Canadian Churches" (Nashville: Abingdon, 2005). The report showed

steep declines in liberal churches, while conservative churches experienced growth.

11. Bob Reeves, "Conservative churches grow while mainline churches struggle," *Lincoln Journal Star,* 19 August 2005, http://journalstar .com/lifestyles/faith-and-values/article_4ab1fe17-57c9-5c81-9cf0 -1a4748e3c13a.html.

12. Dr. Mark Chaves, "National Congregations Study of 1998," University of Arizona. The study finds a gender gap in 57.9 percent of churches that characterize themselves as more conservative, 67.8 percent of churches that are right in the middle, and 72.4 percent of churches that identify themselves as more liberal.

13. Edwin Louis Cole, *Maximized Manhood: A Guide to Family Survival* (New Kensington, PA: Whitaker House, 1982), 166.

14. Gordon Dalbey, *Healing the Masculine Soul: An Affirming Message for Men and the Women Who Love Them* (Dallas: Word Publishing, 1988), 29.

15. Albert L. Winseman, "Congregational Engagement Index: Life Satisfaction and Giving," 26 February 2002, Gallup Tuesday Briefing, Religion and Values Content Channel, www.gallup.com.

16. United Press International, "Study: 'No Religion' Group on Rise," 22 September 2009, http://www.upi.com/Top_News/2009/09/22/ Study-No-religion-group-on-rise/UPI-45631253672675/.

17. Peter Brierley and Heather Wraight, *The Atlas of World Christianity, 2000 Years: Complete Visual Reference to Christianity Worldwide, Including Growth Trends into the New Millennium* (Nashville: Nelson Reference, 1998), 54.

18. "Many Black Men Leaving the Church for the Mosque," *Tennessean* 89, no. 234, posted on the Islamic Bulletin website, www .islamicbulletin.org/newsletters/issue_12/islam.aspx#a4.

Chapter 4: Who Are the Missing Men?

1. D. Michael Lindsay, "A Gated Community in the Evangelical World," *USA Today,* 11 February 2008, page 13A. Also, telephone interview with Dr. Lindsay, 12 March 2011.

2. Camerin Courtney, "O Brother, Where Art Thou?" *Christianity Today,* http://www.crosswalk.com/11621119/.

3. Podles, *The Church Impotent,* 8–9.

4. "A Quick Question: How Religiously Active Are Gay Men?" Hartford Institute for Religion Research, quoting a study by Darren E. Sherkat, professor of sociology, Southern Illinois University,

http://hirr.hartsem.edu/research/quick_question19.html.
5. Matthew 19:29.

Chapter 5: The Masculinity Bank
1. Warren Farrell, *The Myth of Male Power* (New York: Berkley Publishing Group, 1994), 106.
2. For an excellent film on this topic, watch *The Four Feathers*, starring Heath Ledger, Wes Bentley, and Kate Hudson.
3. David D. Gilmore, *Manhood in the Making: Cultural Concepts of Masculinity* (New Haven: Yale University Press, 1990), 11.

Chapter 6: The Two Jesuses
1. Matthew 10:34.
2. See Matthew 16:23; Matthew 15:12; Matthew 11:23.
3. Matthew 15:26.
4. Brandon O'Brien, "A Jesus for Real Men," *Christianity Today*, April 2008, 51–52.
5. Kenny Luck, *Risk: Are You Willing to Trust God with Everything?* (Colorado Springs: WaterBrook Press, 2006); David Platt, *Radical: Taking Back Your Faith from the American Dream* (Sisters, OR: Multnomah, 2010); John Eldredge, *Wild at Heart: Discovering the Secret of a Man's Soul* (Nashville: Thomas Nelson, 2001).
6. Matthew 17:17.
7. John 2:15.
8. See Mark 7:18; 8:33; and Matthew 23:27, among others.
9. Tim Stafford, "The Church's Walking Wounded," *Christianity Today*, March 2003, http://www.christianitytoday.com/ct/2003/march/9.64.html.
10. Romans 2:4.

Chapter 7: Victoria's Secret... When We Lost the Men
1. Dr. Leon Podles, *The Church Impotent: The Feminization of Christianity* (Dallas: Spence Publishing, 1999).
2. Ibid., 19.
3. Ibid., 17.
4. "Sinners in the Hands of an Angry God" was preached on July 8, 1741, in Enfield, Connecticut, by Jonathan Edwards.
5. Ann Douglas, *The Feminization of American Culture* (New York: Alfred E. Knopf, 1977), 100.

6. Clifford Putney, *Muscular Christianity: Manhood and Sports* in *Protestant America, 1880–1920* (Cambridge, MA: Harvard University Press, 2003), 75.

Chapter 8: *The Christian-Industrial Complex*
1. Susan Faludi, *Stiffed: The Betrayal of the American Man* (New York: HarperCollins, 1999), 256.
2. Gene Edward Veith, "You Are What You Read," *World*, July/August 2002, 26.
3. Pat Morley, "Why Don't Men Read Christian Books? Just a Thought . . . ," 6 October 2003, "Man in the Mirror Weekly Briefing" e-newsletter.
4. Shannon Ethridge, *Every Woman's Battle* (Colorado Springs: WaterBrook Press, 2003), back cover.
5. Larry Keefauver, *Lord, I Wish My Husband Would Pray with Me* (Lake Mary, FL: Creation House, 1998), 90.
6. Nancy Kennedy, *When He Doesn't Believe* (Colorado Springs: WaterBrook Press, 2001), 194.
7. Advertisement in *New Man* magazine. The book is called *Kissing the Face of God: Enter a New Realm of Worship More Wonderful than You Can Imagine*, by Sam Hinn (Lake Mary, FL: Creation House, 2002).
8. Barna Research Online, "Christian Mass Media Reach More Adults with the Christian Message than Do Churches," July 2, 2002, www.barna.org.
9. "The Explosion of Christian Music," *Radio & Records*, 19 April 2002, 46.
10. John 12:32.

Chapter 9: *Men and Contemporary Worship*
1. Patrick M. Arnold, *Wildmen, Warriors and Kings: Masculine Spirituality and the Bible* (New York: Crossroad Publishing, 1991), 77.
2. Darrell Evans, "Your Love Is Extravagant," CCLI song no. 2612711. ©1998 Integrity's Hosanna! Music.
3. Arbitron Audience Composition Report, summer 2003, posted at www.arbitron.com. Exact figures: album-oriented rock: men 69 percent, women 27 percent; soft adult contemporary: men 32 percent, women 67 percent.
4. Chuck Swindoll, "The Problem with Pizzazz: Has Entertainment Replaced Scripture as the Center of Our Worship?" *Leadership Journal*, May 2011, http://www.christianitytoday.com/le/2011/spring/problempizzazz.html.

Chapter 10: Twelve Things Men Fear about Church

1. James Dobson, *Bringing Up Boys* (Wheaton: Tyndale, 2001), 25–26. Men have a larger amygdala than women. Some scientists believe this causes men to flash back more easily to traumatic situations.
2. Sam Keene, *Fire in the Belly: On Being a Man* (New York: Bantam Books, 1991), 140.
3. Mark I. Pinsky, "Saint Flanders," *Christianity Today*, February 5, 2001.
4. Mark D. Jordan, "What Attracts Gay Men to the Catholic Priesthood?" *Boston Globe*, 3 May 2002, Section A, 23.
5. J. L. King with Karen Hunter, *On the Down Low: A Journey into the Lives of "Straight" Black Men Who Sleep with Men* (New York: Harlem Moon, 2005), 82–83.
6. *Ministry Today* magazine online, podcast, 5 March 2007. Also see Michael Stevens, *Straight Up: The Church's Official Response to the Epidemic of Downlow Living* (Lake Mary, FL: Creation House, 2007).
7. Jesse Ventura, as quoted at the American Atheists website. http:// en.wikipedia.org/wiki/Jesse_Ventura.
8. Personal conversation with Pastor Mark Gungor, Santa Ana, CA, 14 June 2007.
9. Hayes Carll, "She Left Me for Jesus," 2008, UMG Recordings, Inc.
10. Linda Davis, *How to Be the Happy Wife of an Unsaved Husband* (New Kensington, PA: Whitaker House, 1987), 59.
11. Sabrina D. Black, *Can Two Walk Together? Encouragement for Spiritually Unbalanced Marriages* (Chicago: Lift Every Voice, 2002), 194.
12. Kevin Leman, *Making Sense of the Men in Your Life: What Makes Them Tick, What Ticks You Off, and How to Live in Harmony* (Nashville: Thomas Nelson, 2001), 122.
13. Nancy Wray Gegoire, endorsement of *Why Men Hate Going to Church*, first edition, inside cover.
14. John Ortberg, *Everybody's Normal Till You Get to Know Them* (Grand Rapids: Zondervan, 2003), from the excerpt, "Our Secret Fears About Heaven," *Today's Christian Woman*, July/August 2003, 38.

Chapter 11: The Stars vs. the Scrubs

1. Anne and Bill Moir, *Why Men Don't Iron* (New York: Citadel Press, 1999), 116.
2. Ibid., 135. Moir's source is the *Diagnostic and Statistical Manual of Mental Disorders*, 4th ed. (DSM-IV), American Psychiatric Association (1995), 49.
3. Bruce Weber, "Fewer Noses Stuck in Books in America, Survey Finds," *New York Times*, 8 July 2004.

4. Thom and Joani Schultz, *Why Nobody Learns Much of Anything in Church: And How to Fix It* (Loveland, CO: Group Publishing, 1996), 136.

5. Mike Bergman, "Majority of Undergrads and Graduate Students Are Women, Census Bureau Reports," *US Census Bureau News*, 19 December 2006.

Chapter 12: Check Your Testosterone at the Door

1. Woody L. Davis, "Evangelizing the Pre-Christian Male," Net Results, June 2001, 4, www.netresults.org.

2. Jesus is quoted using the phrases "kingdom of God" or "kingdom of heaven" more than eighty times in the Gospels. The number of times he used the phrase "family of God"? Zero.

3. Stephen W. Smith, *The Transformation of a Man's Heart* (Downers Grove, IL: InterVarsity, 2006), 44.

4. Jawanza Kunjufu, *Adam! Where Are You? Why Most Black Men Don't Go to Church* (Chicago: African American Images, 1997), 94.

Chapter 13: How Churches Feminize Over Time

1. Mark Driscoll, video interview 21 September 2008, Mars Hill Church, Seattle, WA. Watch the video at: http://bit.ly/MarkDriscoll.

Chapter 14: How Churches Drive Boys Away from the Faith

1. "LifeWay Research Uncovers Reasons 18 to 22 Year Olds Drop Out of Church," PowerPoint presentation accompanying study, available at the LifeWay website, http://www.lifeway.com/lwc/article_main_page/0,1703,A=165949&M=200906,00.html.

2. See Matthew 17:18; Mark 5:12–13; John 2:15; and John 8:59.

3. See 1 Corinthians 13:11.

4. Dr. Christian Smith, National Study of Youth and Religion, conducted at the University of North Carolina at Chapel Hill.

5. Drew Dyck, "The Red Bull Gospel," *LeadershipJournal.net*, posted 9 May 2011.

6. Paul Hill, David Anderson, and Roland Martinson, *Coming of Age: Exploring the Spirituality and Identity of Younger Men* (Minneapolis: Augsburg, 2006), 54.

Chapter 15: The Battle to Reengage Men

1. YMCA website, http://www.ymca.net/history/founding.html.
2. Clifford Putney, *Muscular Christianity: Manhood and Sports in Protestant America, 1880-1920* (Cambridge, MA: Harvard University Press, 2003), 59.
3. Ibid, 117.
4. Ibid, 74.
5. Lyle E. Schaller, *It's a Different World: The Challenge for Today's Pastor* (Nashville: Abingdon, 1987), 61–62.
6. Linda Green, "United Methodist death rates higher than U.S. Average." United Methodist Church website, http://www.umc .org/site/apps/nlnet/content3.aspx?c=lwL4KnN1LtH&b=2789393 &ct=7166841.
7. F. D. Huntington, *Sermons for the People* (Boston: Crosby, Nichols & Co, 1856), 350.

Chapter 16: Why Megachurches Are Mega

1. Scott Thuma and Dave Travis, *Beyond Megachurch Myths: What We Can Learn from America's Largest Churches* (New York: Jossey-Bass, 2007), 6.
2. Dr. Mark Chaves, "The National Congregations Study," http://www .soc.duke.edu/natcong/index.html.
3. James B. Twitchell, *Shopping for God: How Christianity Went from In Your Heart to In Your Face* (Simon & Schuster), 249–54.
4. Rick Warren, *The Purpose Driven Church* (Grand Rapids: Zondervan, 1995), 169–71.
5. Lee Strobel, *Inside the Mind of Unchurched Harry and Mary* (Grand Rapids: Zondervan, 1993), 190.
6. Ibid., 189.
7. Bob Russell with Rusty Russell, *When God Builds a Church* (West Monroe, LA: Howard, 2000), 113.

Chapter 17: Pastors and Men

1. Dr. Michael Lindsay, telephone interview, 12 March 2011.
2. Barbara Brown Zikmund, Adair T. Lummis, and Patricia M. Y. Chang, "Women, Men and Styles of Clergy Leadership," *Christian Century*, 6 May 1998, 115, excerpted from *Clergywomen: An Uphill Calling* (Louisville: Westminster John Knox Press, 1998).
3. Patrick Arnold, *Wildmen, Warriors, and Kings: Masculine Spirituality and the Bible* (New York: Crossroad, 1991), 19.

4. Lee Strobel, *Inside the Mind of Unchurched Harry and Mary* (Grand Rapids: Zondervan, 1993), 66.
5. Thom S. Rainer, *Surprising Insights from the Unchurched and Proven Ways to Reach Them* (Grand Rapids: Zondervan, 2001), 60.
6. Jeri Odell, *Spiritually Single: Living with an Unbelieving Husband* (Kansas City: Beacon Hill Press, 2002), 97.
7. Rainer, *Surprising Insights from the Unchurched*, 127, 132, 134.

Chapter 18: Teaching and Men

1. Matthew 7:29.
2. For you trivia buffs, the longest parable in Scripture took me two minutes, twenty seconds to read (Luke 15:11–32). The shortest: five seconds (Matt. 13:33).
3. For more on Christ's sense of humor, read Robert Darden's, *Jesus Laughed: The Redemptive Power of Humor* (Nashville: Abingdon, 2008).
4. Robert Lewis, personal interview, 6 November 2002, Indianapolis.
5. Matthew 7:28.
6. Lewis, personal interview.
7. United States Army recruiting brochure RPI 272, January 2002.
8. See Matthew 12:14; Matthew 15:12; and Luke 4:8.

Chapter 19: Getting the Big Story Right

1. Luke 9:57 CEV.
2. Luke 9:58 CEV.
3. In Matthew 13:3–9, Jesus spoke of four kinds of seed. Only one produced a crop. That's where I got the "fewer than one in four will remain loyal" figure. I realize Christ wasn't speaking with mathematical precision here, but it squares with other passages that indicate that few disciples produce a crop.
4. Matthew 10:41–42.
5. Matthew 19:21.
6. Matthew 19:27 CEV.
7. Matthew 19:28–30 CEV.
8. Thom S. Rainer, *Surprising Insights from the Unchurched and Proven Ways to Reach Them* (Grand Rapids: Zondervan, 2001), 111.
9. Vicki Marsh Kabat, "Old Time Religion . . . Is It Good Enough for You?" *Baylor Magazine*, January/February 2003, 19.

Chapter 20: What About Women?

1. Craig LeMoult, "Why So Few Male Nurses?" Columbia News Service, 18 April 2006, http://jscms.jrn.columbia.edu/cns/2006-04-18/lemoult-malenurses/.

2. Carl Dudley, "Men Sharing the Burden," Hartford Institute for Religion Research website, April/May 1998, http://hirr.hartsem.edu/leadership/dudley_398.html.

3. Sam Keene, Fire in the Belly: On Being a Man (New York: Bantam Books, 1991), 171.

4. "The Outreach 100 Largest & Fastest Growing Churches in America," 2008, http://www.sermoncentral.com/articleb.asp?article=Top-100-Fastest-Growing-Churches.

5. Martin E. Marty, "Women Clergy: The Numbers," Beliefnet, quoting Laura S. Olson, Sue E. S. Crawford, and James L. Guth, "Changing Issue Agendas of Women Clergy," Journal for the Scientific Study of Religion, June 2000.

6. Barbara G. Wheeler, "Is There a Problem? Theological Students and Religious Leadership for the Future," Auburn Studies, Auburn Theological Seminary, July 2001, 5.

7. Dr. Leon Podles, The Church Impotent: The Feminization of Christianity (Dallas: Spence Publishing, 1999), xiii.

8. Christopher Morgan and Sarah Keenlyside, "Women priests take ordination lead over men," Sunday Times, 5 September 2004, http://www.timesonline.co.uk/tol/news/uk/article478635.ece.

9. Dr. Mark Chaves, "The National Congregations Study," http://www.soc.duke.edu/natcong/index.html.

10. Barbara Brown Zikmund, Adair T. Lummis, and Patricia M. Y. Chang, "Women, Men and Styles of Clergy Leadership," Christian Century, 6 May 1998, 115, excerpted from Clergywomen: An Uphill Calling (Louisville: Westminster John Knox Press, 1998).

11. Marty, "Women Clergy: The Numbers."

Chapter 21: Young Men and Faith

1. "A Report on the Crisis in the Catholic Church in the United States," the National Review Board for the Protection of Children and Young People, US Conference of Catholic Bishops, 27 February 2004, 80, http://www.usccb.org/nrb/nrbstudy/nrbreport.htm.

2. Robbie Low, "The Truth About Men & Church," Touchstone, June 2003, http://touchstonemag.com/archives/article.php?id=16-05-024-v.

3. "LifeWay Research Uncovers Reasons 18 to 22 Year Olds Drop Out of Church," PowerPoint presentation accompanying study, available at the LifeWay website, http://www.lifeway.com/lwc/article_main _page/0,1703,A=165949&M=200906,00.html.

4. Robert Lewis, *Raising a Modern-Day Knight* (Carol Stream, IL: Tyndale, 1999).

5. Rick Osborne, *Boys Bible* (NIV), (Grand Rapids: Zonderkidz, 2002), back cover.

6. Biblezines (Nashville: Thomas Nelson, 2008).

7. Chuck Stecker, "Foundations of Christian Leadership," in *Effective Men's Ministry: The Indispensable Toolkit for Your Church*, Phil Downer, ed. (Grand Rapids: Zondervan, 2001), 107.

Chapter 22: Men, Prayer, and a Few Other Things

1. See Matthew 6:7.

2. Dan Schaffer, Building Brothers Newsletter, Fall 2002, www .buildingbrothers.org.

3. Drs. Les and Leslie Parrott, *Saving Your Second Marriage before It Starts: Nine Questions to Ask Before You Remarry* (Grand Rapids: Zondervan, 2001), 176.

4. Matthew 6:7 NIV.

5. Matthew 6:9–13 KJV.

Chapter 23: How Men Minister to Others

1. John Gray, *Men Are from Mars, Women Are from Venus* (New York: HarperCollins, 1992), 42.

2. Eric Swanson, "Blueprint Research: Ten Paradigm Shifts Towards Community Transformation (Part II)," *IntoAction Newsletter*, February 2003.

3. Robert Lewis, personal interview, 6 November 2002, Indianapolis.

4. Adam Hamilton, *Leading Beyond the Walls* (Nashville: Abingdon Press, 2002), 146.

5. Bruce H. Wilkinson, *The Prayer of Jabez* (Sisters, OR: Multnomah, 2000), 47.

6. http://www.bpnews.net/bpnews.asp?id=30161.

7. Pat Morley and David Delk, *Ten Practical Secrets to Attract and Retain Men*, a brochure from Man in the Mirror Ministries, 2002.

8. Rick Warren, *The Purpose Driven Church* (Grand Rapids: Zondervan, 1995), 387.

9. Pat Morley, "The Distinction Between Disciples and Workers," Man in the Mirror *Weekly Briefing* e-newsletter, September 15, 2003, 48,

www.maninthemirror.org/weekly-briefing
/the-distinction-between-disciples-and-workers.

Chapter 24: How to Minister to Men
1. All quotes from Mark Driscoll in this chapter are taken from a
video interview I conducted, 21 September 2008, Mars Hill Church,
Seattle, WA.
2. Albert L. Winseman, "Religion and Gender: A Congregation
Divided, Part II," December 10, 2002, Gallup Tuesday Briefing,
Religion and Values Content Channel, www.gallup.com.
3. Dan Erickson and Dan Schaffer, "Modern Man in Contemporary
Culture," in *Effective Men's Ministry: The Indispensable Toolkit for Your
Church*, Phil Downer, ed. (Grand Rapids: Zondervan, 2001), 18.
4. 1 Corinthians 4:14–15.
5. For more information about Steve Sonderman and his *Top Gun*
curriculum, see www.topgunministries.org.

Chapter 25: A Church for Everyone
1. Matthew 23:13 NIV.
2. Beth Redman and Matt Redman, "Let My Words Be Few," CCLI
song no. 3040980. ©2000 Thankyou Music.
3. John Buckeridge, "Beautiful News," *Christianity Magazine*, March 2007.
4. Linda Green, "United Methodist Death Rates Higher than Average,"
United Methodist Church website, www.umc.org, 2 July 2009.

About the Author

DAVID MURROW IS AN AWARD-WINNING TELEVISION PRODUCER and writer based in Alaska. (You've probably heard of his most famous former client, Sarah Palin.) He is the director of Church for Men, an organization that helps congregations reconnect with the world's largest unreached people group. The first edition of *Why Men Hate Going to Church* was an instant Christian bestseller, with more than 100,000 copies in print. His efforts have spawned articles in the *New York Times*, the *Wall Street Journal*, and the *Chicago Tribune*, to name a few. He has been featured on PBS, the *NBC Nightly News*, and the Fox News Channel, talking about the gender gap. David is married with three children, two grandchildren, and a dachshund named Pepper.

the MAP

The Way of All Great Men

DAVID MURROW

Author of *Why Men Hate Going to Church*

A map, written in code and hidden in the gospel of
Matthew, reveals a truth so explosive it could rock the
foundations of Christianity – or lead to its rebirth.

Printed in the USA
CPSIA information can be obtained
at www.ICGtesting.com
JSHW031910220424
61653JS00015B/316